In loving memory of my father, Michael Corey Sr., whose strength, benevolence, and courage in the face of adversity will always be an inspiration to me.

Acknowledgments

I would like to thank the following people for assisting in the production of this book:

Mike and Jeanette Corey, Johnny and Danny Corey, David Griffin, John Sanford, Robert Newman, Keith Ward, Father Olof Scott, John Hick, Talal Alhazmi and family, Nahia, Elliot, Janice, Brandon, Eli, Ebie, Sammy, Martha Mae, Jordan, Debbie, Ellen, Henry, Claire, Angie, Kevin, Greg, Zigman and the Zigurats, Al, Eric Marienthal, Gina, Joyce, Rob, Stewart, Steve Levine, Julie, Jeff Lorder, Chick Corea, Al Dimeola, Frank Gambale, Russ Freeman, Carlos, Sloburn, FZ, Uncle Lihum, Cecilia, Paula, Elizabeth, Beth, Dina, Lee, Tracey, Dr. Zekan and staff, Dr. Baxas, Francis, Steve, Sandy, Michele, Mary Parker Townshend, John Townshend, Lauren, Mr. and Mrs. Parker and family, Charlotte, Bonnie, Penny, George Karl, Steve Davis, Helen Hudson, Father George Mitchell, Julie Kirsch, John Sisk, Jeannie Coghill, Michele Harris, and Robert Johnson.

Contents

Chapter One: INTRODUCTION 1

Chapter Two: JONAH AND THE UNCONSCIOUS 5

History or Allegory?, 5
A Psychological Analysis of the Book of Jonah, 6
The Identity of the Shadow, 12
Repression and the Concept of Demon Possession, 15
The Storm, 16
Significance of the Fish, 22
The Prayer, 23
The Mission to Nineveh, 25
A Theodicy for Natural Evils, 30

Chapter Three: JOB 37

The Story of Job, 37
The Relationship Between Knowledge and Evil, 58
Job's Goodness and the Nature of Evil, 64
The Nature of Hell, 78
A Developmental View of Salvation, 84
Eliphaz's First Speech, 91
Job's Reply, 93
God's Response to Job, 96
Contingency, Necessity, and the Ultimate
Transformation of Evil into Good, 99

Chapter Four: EVIL IN THE OLD TESTAMENT 105

Evil, Monotheism, and the Divine Goodness, 106
A Developmental Interpretation of Evil, 113

Chapter Five: ANSWER TO JUNG 116

Jung and the God of the Old Testament, 116

Why Bad Things Happen to Good People, 117
A Pluralistic View of Salvation, 119
Jung's View of Job, 121
The Power of Doubt, 122
The Severity of the Developmental Process, 127
Could God Have Done Better?, 128
The Image and Likeness of God, 139
Jung, Evil, and the Trinity, 140
The Incarnation, 141
Conclusion, 142

BIBLIOGRAPHY 144

INDEX 147

ABOUT THE AUTHOR 151

CHAPTER ONE
Introduction

The Bible is one of the most thoroughly metaphorical books ever written. Within this metaphorical tradition, much of the underlying meaning of this ancient work has been shown to be related to the psychology of human development. Fritz Kunkel, John A. Sanford, and C.G. Jung, among others, have written extensively about this intriguing relationship between psychology and the Judeo-Christian faith, and their findings have been nothing short of remarkable.

These writers have concentrated primarily on the role of the unconscious in human development, and on the Bible's theological treatment of this fascinating partnership. This is as it should be, because the unconscious is now recognized to be the spiritual foundation of the Self, upon which the ego is able to grow towards its eventual goal of self-actualization, or full character development.[1]

This conclusion would have greatly disturbed the modern founder of depth psychology, Sigmund Freud, who originally conceived of the unconscious, not as the psychological vehicle through which God can act in the world, but rather as the ultimate source of religious feeling in human life. Freud argued that it was primarily the unconscious (along with the many existential dilemmas of human existence) that drove human beings to invent a God in their own image, so they could subsequently derive safety and security from Him. This is why Freud considered any sort of theism to be objectively false, and why he believed that committed theists were seriously being deceived by their own minds.

To a certain limited extent, of course, Freud was correct: the unconscious *is* in fact intimately related to most religious phenomena throughout the world. Part of the reason for this, according to Jung, is that the unconscious is numinous, or spiritually oriented, by its very nature. It possesses an immense storehouse of symbolic images, ranging from those in each individual's personal unconscious to those in humankind's collective unconscious, and this allegedly explains why the human mind tends to view the world in terms of transcendent spiritual imagery. But this doesn't necessarily mean that the mind's various symbolic proclivities *fully* account for our perception of the numinous. To the contrary, a God-filled spiritual world can still objectively exist *along side* our cognitive predisposition to view the world in spiritual terms.

Indeed, many religious writers have argued that the unconscious may in fact represent the psychospiritual interface between the human world and the Divine. To the extent that this is true, it would make the unconscious an active *participant* in objective religious truth, and not merely a substitute for it. In response to this fascinating possibility, a growing number of theologians and depth psychologists have concluded that Freud probably went too far in his assertion that the unconscious is the ultimate source of religious feeling in human life.

We can cite two additional reasons for this conclusion. First, there is no way that Freud's atheistic theory can possibly be shown to be objectively true in the absence of an empirical disproof for the existence of God, and this is something that will clearly never be accomplished by finite intellects alone.[2] Secondly, it is becoming increasingly clear that the intra-psychic dynamics surrounding the unconscious are entirely consistent with a religious point of view. Many accomplished authors, including C.G. Jung and John A. Sanford, have convincingly demonstrated that the single most effective means of interpreting religious phenomena is in terms of the unconscious, especially when it comes to the role of this important psychic element in facilitating human development.

Freud's radical opinion about the objective validity of religion seems to have been based, at least in part, on a false inference from a known set of psychological truths. These truths are centered around the profound need of the human mind to believe in a transcendent father-figure, which is evidenced by the fact that virtually all human societies have professed belief in some type of supernatural being over the millennia. Freud simply saw this need as emanating directly out of the mind's desire to escape from its horrible existential plight in the world.

To a certain extent, of course, Freud was absolutely correct: human beings *are* in point of fact the only creatures on this planet who are consciously aware of their own impending doom, and this understandably causes them to experience a tremendous amount of existential anxiety. They stick out like a sore thumb from the rest of creation because they are the only creatures who have been blessed—or cursed—with the miracle of self-consciousness. This awareness, according to Freud, is so overwhelmingly painful and fear-inspiring that human beings are naturally driven to create a God in their own image so they can obtain salvation and redemption from Him, thereby quelling their enormous life and death anxieties.

In short, Freud believed that humans are unconsciously driven to project their need for a transcendent father-figure onto cosmic reality itself, where it is then falsely perceived as a genuine deity. For Freud, then, it was no mere coincidence that most of the world's religions have corresponded so perfectly with humanity's existential needs and fears in the world; this is,

Introduction 3

after all, precisely what would be expected from self-conscious beings who are thoroughly mortified by their existential burden in life.

In other words, Freud correctly surmised that the human mind has an intrinsic need to believe in some type of Supreme Being; so much so, in fact, that if such a Being didn't objectively exist He would have to be invented. *But it is precisely here that Freud went wrong, because it doesn't necessarily follow from this realization that religion must therefore be objectively false.* That is to say, just because we have a profound intrapsychic need for God, and are even capable of creating one to fulfill our own existential need, *doesn't* necessarily mean that God is a fiction. To the contrary, it could just as easily be argued that we need God so desperately precisely *because* we were originally created to exist in spiritual communion with Him. To be sure, if God is truly responsible for creating us, we shouldn't be surprised to find that we need Him in order to be able to function properly. St. Augustine recognized this intimate relationship between God and the human mind over 15 centuries ago, as the following quote well illustrates:

> Thou hast made us for thyself, and our hearts are restless till they rest in thee.

Far from representing an objective appraisal of religion, then, we see that Freud's inference about the non-existence of God was based more on his own biased opinion than it was genuine scientific research or rigorous logic. It should therefore *never* be taken to represent an empirical statement about the role of the unconscious in the genesis of religious faith. Indeed, the competing theistic interpretation—which sees the unconscious, not so much as a substitute for God, but rather as God's world-based means for helping us become fully individuated[3] in the world—appears to be a much more compelling explanation overall, because it accounts for the known evidence much more effectively than does its atheistic counterpart. This being the case, it behooves us to take a deeper look at this intriguing relationship between God and the human psyche, because this is where the underlying meaning of life—the "pearl of great price"—will in all likelihood be found. It is also where the origin of moral evil is likely to be found as well, because most evil actions are known to emanate directly out of the mind's own unconscious depths.

We will begin our study of religion and the unconscious by taking an indepth look at two of the most metaphorical books in the Bible, Job and Jonah. Our goal will be to decipher their hidden meaning in terms of the principles of modern depth psychology, so we can learn all we can from their timeless legacy of wisdom.

Notes

1. The Self can be defined as the center of the total personality. This is why it is also sometimes called the Center in Jungian-style analytical psychology.
2. Finite intellects will never be able to obtain an empirical disproof of God's existence because such a conclusion is only tenable if the entire realm of cosmic knowledge is first analyzed for God's possible existence, and this is something that finite minds can never do by definition. Paradoxically, then, the only being who is epistemologically qualified to make such an absolute statement is God Himself!
3. In speaking of God's acting in human affairs, I don't mean to imply that God acts as an *efficient cause* to bring about certain affairs in the world. Rather, God seems to act as the spiritual and metaphysical foundation of human life, upon which man can subsequently interject his own efficient causes into the world system.

CHAPTER TWO
Jonah and the Unconscious

The book of Jonah contains one of the most exciting and intriguing stories in the entire Bible. It is a deeply symbolic work that was written around the year 760 BC, probably by Jonah himself. Although it is a short book, it contains a wealth of metaphorical wisdom about the role of the unconscious in human development. It can therefore be a tremendous help to us in our attempt to construct a new psychologically-based theology of human development.

History or Allegory?

Before we move on, the question of the actual historicity of the book of Jonah needs to be briefly addressed. While most Biblical scholars would agree that this story was never meant to be taken literally, many people nevertheless fail to take it seriously because they find it exceedingly hard to believe that a person could actually survive for three days and three nights within the belly of a giant "fish."

For the sake of these individuals, it should be pointed out that it is a zoological fact that humans can survive quite nicely for brief periods within the large air-filled cavities of giant whales (which were called "fish" in Old Testament days). Indeed, there have been a number of reports over the years of people being consumed by whales and surviving. One man off the coast of Hawaii, for instance, is said to have been swallowed alive by a whale while swimming in the Pacific Ocean. He was able to survive for some 48 hours inside of the whale before he was expelled again in one piece into the sea.

Although this anecdotal report admittedly sounds far-fetched, three factors conspire together to make this sort of thing a real-world possibility. First, whales are not carnivorous. In spite of their large size, they only eat microscopic plankton, not human-sized pieces of flesh. In order to do this, however, they must skim the sea for hours at a time with their mouths open so they can absorb enough plankton to live on. It is therefore quite possible that a whale could accidentally "swallow" a human being while skimming the ocean for plankton.

Moreover, since whales aren't designed to eat human-sized pieces of meat, they aren't likely to swallow a person who has inadvertently been ingested. Instead, whales possess a huge air-filled cavity inside their heads, which functions to store air for the whale during deep sea dives (whales, you will recall, are mammals and not fish, so they breathe air just like we do). It is quite possible, then, that a person who has been inadvertently swallowed by a whale could subsequently be channeled into this air-filled cavity, which would contain more than enough air and room to support the life of a human being for a brief time.

Finally, it is quite plausible that such an individual could be redeposited back into the sea in a biologically intact state whenever the whale was ready to do so. If and when this ever occurred, of course, the individual would then be faced with the prodigious task of trying to find his or her way back to shore.

It is thus distinctly possible that a historical man by the name of Jonah could indeed have been swallowed by a whale long ago, only to be expelled three days later in one piece. But even if such a thing were not technically feasible, we would nevertheless be compelled to recognize that the entire story of Jonah is supposed to be understood as a Divine Miracle, and miracles are generally taken to represent events that lie outside the realm of normal causation.

But even if one still insists on denying the actual historicity of Jonah's experience inside the whale, this wonderful little book nevertheless contains a wealth of deeply symbolic material that is directly applicable to many of the spiritual troubles that afflict us today. Indeed, as far as most modern Biblical scholars are concerned, it is in this deeper allegorical sense that the majority of the Bible is supposed to have its true meaning. The British philosopher John Hick, for instance, believes that Biblical myths are "true" stories about the human condition, regardless of whether or not they ever actually occurred in the real world. For Hick, then, the story of Jonah can be entirely "true" even if it never actually happened.

A Psychological Analysis of the Book of Jonah

The story of Jonah begins with God making a direct behavioral appeal to the feisty prophet:

> The word of the Lord came to Jonah son of Amittai: "Go to the great city of Nineveh and preach against it, because its wickedness has come up before me" (Jonah 1:1–2).[1]

We can, of course, understand the meaning of this passage in an entirely literal fashion, as most readers are probably inclined to do. However, it is also possible to look at it in an allegorical fashion as well, so that its various elements can then become symbolic of the more hidden, psychological aspects of human life. The character of Jonah, for instance, can be seen as representing the ego, while the wickedness of the city of Nineveh can be seen as representing the pathological aspects of the mind's various repressed elements. Similarly, the word of the Lord can be seen as representing the instinctual urgings of the inner Self, which is the integrative center of the human soul. It can also be seen as representing the final state of existential justice in the world.

From this allegorical point of view, the first two verses of the book of Jonah can be understood to represent the inner dialogue between the Self and the ego, in which the Self is perpetually trying to persuade the ego into acquiring a state of psychospiritual wholeness for itself. Similarly, the "word of the Lord" that came to Jonah can be understood as representing the Self's inner drive to wholeness that is present in all persons. Its function is to urge the ego into facing the unwanted aspects of the unconscious mind, because as Jung and others have pointed out, the human personality cannot be fully integrated until *all* of its constituent parts have been reunited into a seamless whole. The problem of moral evil also cannot be properly dealt with until this momentous act of integration takes place, because the constant state of psychological repression that is required to keep these rejected elements at bay inevitably tends to distort the mind's higher cognitive and emotional centers into a pathological, maladaptive state, which in turn tends to generate a significant amount of wickedness in a person's life. One of the most unfortunate consequences of this internal lack of congruence is that it tends to thwart any further growth of the personality.

Jung's analytic psychology supports us in this interpretation, for it tells us that there is a strange, subterranean aspect of the human mind known as the *Shadow*, which contains the despised and rejected elements of the personality. Because of its highly feared contents, the Shadow is instinctively imprisoned within the realm of the unconscious, so that it cannot openly disturb the day-to-day functioning of the ego.

The beginning of the story of Jonah is thus metaphorically concerned with a reconciliation between the ego and its rejected Shadow. From this Jungian point of view, the wickedness of the city of Nineveh can be understood to represent the "wickedness" that is inevitably generated when the unwanted aspects of the personality are banished to the unconscious, while the physical distance between Jonah and the city of Nineveh can be understood to represent the tremendous psychological gulf that separates the conscious ego from the unconscious mind itself.

Now, there is a fundamental drive at work in the human mind that is mediated by the Self, which acts to promote wholeness by opposing the splintering and subsequent repression of any part of the personality. It has been called the urge for *individuation* by Jung and the drive for *self-actualization* by Abraham Maslow. As a direct consequence of this inner drive, whenever we try to get rid of a major part of ourselves by repressing it into the unconscious, that part tends to resurface again with a vengeance later on, so that it can hopefully be reintegrated back within the matrix of the larger personality. In fact, this is the proximate source for much of the moral evil that takes place in our world, for anytime we selfishly try to destroy an essential part of ourselves for our own personal convenience, that forsaken part tends to wreak a great deal of havoc with us later on. The ego, in turn, characteristically responds to this divisive act of repression by behaving in an irrational and destructive manner, thereby increasing the burden of moral evil in the world.

Jesus was well aware of the importance and validity of this inner psychological law, as the following quote well illustrates:

> Every kingdom divided against itself is brought to desolation, and every city or house divided against itself will not stand (Matt. 12:25).

While this passage undoubtedly has an outer meaning, it also has an inner, psychological meaning that is of primary interest to us here. Jesus is telling us that the inner "house" of the personality cannot possibly stand or exist in a healthy manner as long as it is divided against itself. What this means in modern terms is that the conscious mind cannot remain opposed to the unconscious Shadow for very long, or else the entire personality will eventually self-destruct.

There is a verse in the apocryphal Gospel of Thomas that seems to relate directly to the problem of the Shadow in human life:

> Jesus said, "If you bring forth what is within you, what you have will save you. If you do not have that within you, what you do not have within you [will] kill you" (v. 70).[2]

In this intriguing passage Jesus seems to be referring to the hidden elements of the personality that have been banished to the unconscious. In this way of thinking, if we are able to "bring forth" these repressed elements into the larger matrix of our conscious personality, the resulting wholeness will save us because it will make us fit for the kingdom of God. On the other hand, if we are not able to bring forth or reintegrate these rejected elements, the resulting character disintegration will eventually kill us through any number of different self-destructive mechanisms.

In yet another passage from the Gospel of Thomas, Jesus makes this point perfectly clear:

> I am the one who comes from what is whole. I was given from the things of my father. . . . For this reason I say, if one is whole, one will be filled with light, but if one is divided, one will be filled with darkness (v. 61).[3]

One will be filled with light if one is whole because psychospiritual wholeness is the chief prerequisite for mental and emotional health; it is also vitally important for personal happiness and productivity as well. On the other hand, if one's innermost soul is divided against itself, one will be filled with the darkness of neurosis, which is very dark indeed.

The Parable of the Lost Coin reiterates this basic theme of psychological redemption in a most interesting way:

"Suppose a woman has ten silver coins and loses one. Does she not light a lamp, sweep the house and search carefully until she finds it? And when she finds it, she calls her friends and neighbors together and says, 'Rejoice with me; I have found my lost coin.' In the same way, I tell you, there is rejoicing in the presence of the angels of God over one sinner who repents" (Luke 15:8–9).

This parable also has an internal meaning associated with it, as John Sanford points out in *The Kingdom Within*.[4] On this inner, psychological level, the complete set of ten silver coins can be seen to represent our goal of psychological wholeness, whereas the lost coin can be seen to represent the lost parts of ourselves. This is why the lost coin is so exceedingly important: because it is absolutely necessary to restore a sense of completeness to the original ten-member set, just as *all* of our internal repressions need to be reclaimed before our personality can be truly whole. No wonder the woman is so overjoyed when she finds her lost coin: because this represents the overwhelming happiness that we will all eventually experience when we finally integrate the Shadow and become ontologically complete human beings.

Interestingly enough, it is the Spirit of God, acting through the inner urgings of the Self, that tries to push the mind's unconscious elements back towards consciousness. It is also the Spirit of God, acting through the Self, that calls for an inner act of reconciliation between the ego and its Shadow. It does this in order to promote the redemption of the lost parts of the personality, so that the individual can subsequently become whole and thereby be initiated into the kingdom of heaven.

This appears to be a major reason why the Bible blames the Spirit of God for causing so much of the destructiveness in human life. For by pushing the unwanted contents of the Shadow towards consciousness, the inner Spirit of God (disguised as the Self) is able to generate a tremendous amount of turmoil within the mind, which in turn tends to manifest itself in the external world in the form of irrational and destructive behaviors. The ego, of course, wants nothing at all to do with the Shadow, but the Spirit of God, in its perennial quest for wholeness, relentlessly tries to stir up trouble anyway by continually urging the ego to come to terms with its psychological enemy.

This in fact appears to be the meaning behind Jesus' enigmatic saying that He didn't come to bring peace on the earth but a sword (Luke 10:34).

Indeed, it is for this very reason that the neurotic personality is often depressed and anxiety-stricken: because the ascent of the Shadow towards consciousness is typically experienced as a dark and foreboding threat. It is a threat because the entire point of the neurotic character structure, as Becker, Janov and others have astutely pointed out, is to deny the existence of its own repressions; therefore, any upward movement of the Shadow directly threatens the neurotic personality's entire *raison d'être*.

In order to quell this inner threat, the ego must constantly "de-press" the burgeoning Shadow in order to keep it comfortably at bay. This requires a tremendous amount of psychic effort in order to be successful, which explains why most depressives feel exhausted so much of the time. They feel exhausted because they are burning an immense amount of energy every day of their lives trying to keep their inner house divided, but even the most heroic repressive effort in the world is bound to fail from time to time. When this happens, the ego inevitably finds itself in partial contact with its own repressed feelings, and it is this partial contact that produces the feeling of de-pression.

Ernest Becker has called this internal psychic division the "vital lie of character," because he recognizes that the entire point of the neurotic's inner life is to keep these repressions out of consciousness at all cost.[5] Unfortunately for the ego, however, this is the very thing that these repressed elements are always trying to do, because their natural inclination is to re-enter consciousness, just as the natural inclination of a submerged piece of cork is to rise to the surface. As a consequence, the neurotic ego has little choice but to perpetually fight against these repressions in whatever way it finds best. This is undoubtedly why the neurotic feels mentally and emotionally drained so much of the time: because he is unknowingly fighting the greatest "turf battle" of them all 24 hours a day.

In his Pulitzer Prize-winning book *The Denial of Death*, Ernest Becker grapples with this inner psychological dilemma in a particularly heroic fashion, and eventually comes to the same momentous conclusion that had been reached a century earlier by the Danish existential philosopher Søren Kierkegaard; namely, that the mind's repressions need to be confronted and reintegrated back into the personality at all cost. Unfortunately, this process of self-reintegration is much easier said than done, because it necessarily entails a shedding of one's neurotic "character armor," so that one can then face the realities of life entirely on their own terms. Very few people, however, can stand naked in the storm of life in this fashion and survive without some larger foundation to fall back on. This, according to Becker, is God's role in the self-transforming process. Indeed, God is the *only* Being who can support us in this capacity, because He alone possesses transcendent power over life and death.

It is precisely here that Kierkegaard's famous "leap of faith" comes into play. For instead of trembling helplessly in the face of his innermost pains and fears, the self-transforming individual is supposed to take the required leap of faith in the direction of self-reintegration, trusting exclusively in the power of God to sustain him, for only then will his repressions be able to cease their wicked contribution to the neurotic process.

At the same time, though, God cannot be unduly blamed for inciting this type of intra-psychic conflict, because He is only trying to work for our eventual good by attempting to bring the warring factions within our minds back together again. In the meantime, however, this internal peace initiative only seems to create more problems for the ego, because it is primarily concerned with pushing the Shadow in the very direction it doesn't want to go, which in turn tends to generate a tremendous amount of pain and destructiveness in a person's life.

The profound wickedness of the city of Nineveh can thus be understood to represent the pathological wickedness that is inevitably generated whenever the Shadow is repressed. Indeed, this wickedness is so great that God tells Jonah that He will destroy the entire city if it doesn't repent. This is directly symbolic of the profound self-destruction that will eventually take place in an individual's life if the ego doesn't come to terms with its Shadow. And the sooner this peace initiative takes place the better, because the evil that is caused by the Shadow can quickly get out of hand if it isn't nipped in the bud. It can even threaten the physical survival of the entire Self if it is allowed to go too far, just as God threatened to destroy the entire city of Nineveh if it didn't repent.

We see, then, that God's command for Jonah to preach to the people of Nineveh is directly symbolic of the Self's relentless push for reconciliation within the mind. It continually tries to persuade the ego to "preach" to the contents of the unconscious because it wants these "evil" elements to "repent," so that they can in turn be reintegrated within the overall gestalt of the personality. For once these repressed elements are duly faced and appropriately dealt with, they will then be able to be safely reintegrated into the larger personality structure, because at that point they will have largely been stripped of their destructive power.

In typically human fashion, though, Jonah refuses to heed the Lord's command, and chooses instead to flee to Tarshish (in the south of Spain) by way of boat:

> But Jonah ran away from the Lord and headed for Tarshish. He went down to Joppa, where he found a ship bound for that port. After paying the fare, he went aboard and sailed for Tarshish to flee from the Lord (Jonah 1:3).

This verse clearly symbolizes the tendency of the cowardly ego to run away from the stern warnings that are repeatedly issued by the Self. The reason for this tendency, as Freud and others have pointed out, is that the immature ego tends to operate primarily on the pleasure principle, so it wants to attain nothing more than its own immediate self-interest, which it idiosyncratically defines in terms of whatever happens to feel best. This is why the ego tends to do all it possibly can to avoid the mind's repressions in the first place: because it perceives them in the most unpleasant, aversive terms imaginable.

The Self, on the other hand, yearns for wholeness. It is a teleologically-oriented spiritual entity, so it is primarily interested in seeing the personality reach its own full development.[6] However, the Self also knows that the repressed contents of the unconscious need to be directly confronted and reintegrated back into the personality before this teleological goal can be reached, so it does everything in its power to make this happen. The ego, on the other hand, is typically afraid to follow the Self's command, because it is utterly terrified of its own repressions. As a consequence, the ego struggles incessantly to maintain the psychic *status quo*, which attempts to keep the mind's repressions perpetually at bay.

The Identity of the Shadow

As far as the specific internal identity of the Shadow itself is concerned, numerous theorists have concluded that it is comprised of three principal ingredients: 1) the despised elements of the personality that have been repressed out of consciousness, 2) the idiosyncratic emotional traumas of childhood that were too painful to be fully admitted into consciousness, and 3) the twin existential fears of life and death, which so overwhelm the mind that they must be banished to the unconscious in order to preserve the individual's equanimity in the world.

All three of these psychic elements are experienced in such a profoundly aversive manner by the ego that they are instinctively imprisoned within the unconscious as a protective mechanism. In other words, the mind, rather than disintegrating in the face of all of its dreadful pains and fears, automatically opts to defend its integrity by thrusting these unwanted psychic elements down into the unconscious, where they won't be directly perceived by the ego. Ironically, though, this short-term act of self-preservation eventually ends up threatening the health and coherence of the individual in the long run through a number of different psychopathological mechanisms, all of which are growth-inhibiting by their very nature.

Even so, the Shadow's contribution to the personality doesn't appear to be all bad. To the contrary, this subterranean aspect of the mind also seems to provide a major source of psychic energy for the individual. It is this diffuse psychic energy that enables the personality to be strong, decisive, and clever in the face of negative input from without. Taken by itself, though, this aspect of the Shadow appears to be aversive and even virulent, but in the context of the entire personality this negative quality quickly vanishes, only to be replaced by a beneficial psychic force that is vital to the continued growth and well-being of the entire person.

It is important to note, however, that the strength-infusing aspects of the Shadow aren't necessarily identical with the different repressions that it contains. While these repressions may reside within the Shadow, and may even help to infuse it with much of its underlying power, they *don't* seem to be one and the same with the larger Shadow itself. I say this because it doesn't appear as though the power-infusing aspects of the Shadow will dissipate once the mind's repressions have been purged from the unconscious. If this were true, then this purgative process would ultimately be undesirable and even catastrophic, since it would also cause the personality's power and effectiveness to simultaneously dry up. Rather, the intrinsic character of the mind's shadow realm appears to be energetic and powerful in and of itself, quite apart from any repressed thoughts or feelings *per se*.

Nowhere has the Shadow's overall importance been more graphically illustrated than in one of the old "Star Trek" episodes, where a technical malfunction in the transporter room causes Captain Kirk to spontaneously divide into two distinctly different selves: a sheepishly benign "good" self, and a horribly malignant "evil" self. The "good" Kirk can readily be seen to be indicative of what the human personality would be like in the absence of the Shadow's energizing elements, whereas the "evil" Kirk can be seen to be indicative of the Shadow personality itself, apart from any association with the individual's larger character structure. This division clearly illustrates how important the Shadow is to the whole human being, because the "good" Kirk is clearly too frail and weak to be able to accomplish anything substantive in his life, even though he is totally "good" in terms of his underlying motivational state. The "evil" Kirk, on the other hand, is full of strength and resolve, but his behavior isn't tempered by anything positive or constructive, so he continually works for evil.

In short, the two Kirks desperately need one another before they can function effectively on the Enterprise, just as the "good" ego needs the "evil" Shadow's energizing powers before it can be strong enough to have a significant impact on the world. This means that the Shadow is only evil as long as it is abstracted out of the context of the entire personality. Within the gestalt of the larger character structure, though, it suddenly becomes transformed into a good force.

There are two additional conclusions that we can draw from this ontological division of Kirk's personality. First, the evil aspects of the Shadow, when taken alone, appear to be indivisible from its strength-infusing aspects. This would seem to be one reason why human beings are so prone to evil at the present time: because the mind's inner source of psychic strength also appears to have some degree of evil necessarily associated with it, at least temporarily. In a fully developed person, of course, this "evil" side isn't a problem, because the higher aspects of the personality function to direct these evil tendencies exclusively towards good ends. When this takes place, the Shadow's "evil" side makes a valuable contribution to the larger personality, since it gives the mind the power and decisiveness to be maximally effective in life. Within this context of optimal psychic maturity, the Shadow clearly isn't evil at all; it is good.

Indeed, this is one of the main reasons why a lack of character maturity is able to contribute so extensively to the genesis of moral evil in the world: because morally immature individuals aren't yet able to exert a significant moderating influence on their own lower psychic influences, which are diffuse, and therefore undirected, by their very nature. In other words, it is the developmental abstraction of the Shadow away from any significant moderating influence that causes it to be evil, because the unactualized human character structure doesn't yet possess enough practical knowledge or moral fiber to be able to direct the intrinsic power of the Shadow exclusively towards good ends. This is one of the main reasons why the personality's goal of individuation is so inherently valuable: because it promises to keep the behavioral production of evil to an absolute minimum, through the development of a higher behavioral regulatory center within the mind.

At this point the reader may be wondering why the personality's energy source has to naturally gravitate towards evil to begin with when it is uncontrolled by the faculties of the higher self. The answer to this question comes from the very nature of diffuse and undirected energy, because any type of *random* behavioral burst can almost be guaranteed to produce some degree of disorganization, and hence evil, in a person's life, simply by virtue of the fact that there are so many more ways to produce evil than good. The higher aspects of the personality are thus required to direct its underlying energy source towards exclusively good ends.

This process of behavioral regulation in analogous to the conditions that are necessary to generate order within physical systems. It is a well-known fact that physical particles, when left to themselves, will always tend to become more disorganized with the passage of time because of the Second Law of Thermodynamics, which states that disorder will always tend to increase in closed physical systems, due to the vast preponderance of disordered states over ordered states, and the implicit assumption that unconstrained physical systems will always tend to behave in a random fashion. Hence, before an ordered state can come into being, some type of larger constraining force is necessary to guide randomly moving particles *away* from their natural inclination towards disorder, and *towards* a more highly ordered state.

In the same way, the natural inclination of unconstrained psychic energy is to become more disordered, and hence more destructive, with the passage of time. This is because the very lack of external constraint naturally entails a certain degree of randomness to the resulting behavior, and any type of random movement virtually guarantees that some type of disorder will eventually result, again because there are so many more disordered states possible than ordered states. This explains why a larger constraining force is necessary within the mind to regularly produce behavioral good: because there is no other way to ensure, given the vast preponderance of disordered over ordered states, that only those states that are ordered, and hence good, will routinely be chosen.

Of course, I am equating goodness with a state of order here and badness with a state of disorder, but this equation doesn't hold up under scrutiny unless one simultaneously blends the orienting force of morality into the overall concept of the good, because horrendous evils are still possible in a highly ordered state, as the mere existence of the highly organized Nazi war machine during WW II makes perfectly clear. However, if one includes the orienting concept of morality into one's overall view of behavioral order, the analogy with the Second Law of Thermodynamics holds.

Repression and the Concept of Demon Possession

It is interesting to note at this point that the mind's repressions have a great deal in common with the Biblical concept of demon possession, because they too are known to possess the soul in a relentless death grip, and they too are capable of bringing about all manner of evil in a person's life. Like demons, our repressions are incorporeal entities, so they cannot be seen, heard, tasted, or touched. They inhabit the spiritual world of the human psyche, so they are intertwined within the innermost recesses of our souls, which explains why they are able to possess us so completely. Significantly, though, their stranglehold on the personality will never cease until they are all reintegrated back within the matrix of the larger personality.

Not coincidentally, this is precisely the same strategy that the Bible advocates for dealing with demon possession. We are repeatedly told throughout the scriptures to resist the many evil influences in our lives so we can achieve self-purification, but we aren't told exactly how to do this. According to the principles of modern depth psychology, however, we can achieve our spiritual goal by coming to terms with our inner enemy as soon as possible, so it can be safely reintegrated within the larger matrix of our personality. Jesus advocated this same strategy in a cryptic passage that is often misunderstood:

> Come to terms with your opponent in good time while you are still on the way to the court with him, or he may hand you over to the judge and the judge to the officer, and you will be thrown into prison. I tell you solemnly, you will not get out till you have paid the last penny (Luke 12:57–59).

Jesus is symbolically advising us here to come to terms with our inner repressions as soon as we possibly can. Otherwise, they will eventually imprison us, and we won't be able to escape until we have faced and reintegrated every last one of them.

Unfortunately, the neurotic tendency of the ego is to run away from the inner callings of the Self, just as Jonah ran away from the Lord's command to preach to the wicked city of Nineveh. This lack of courage on the part of the ego is almost certainly responsible for generating much of the moral evil that exists in our world, because a mind that is constantly running away from its own internal reality can't help but malfunction from time to time, and it is this very malfunctioning that is responsible for generating most destructive behaviors.

The Storm

Once Jonah makes it out to sea, the Lord sends a huge storm to buffet the ship:

> Then the Lord sent a great wind on the sea, and such a violent storm arose that the ship threatened to break up. All the sailors were afraid and each cried out to his own god. And they threw the cargo into the sea to lighten the ship (Jonah 1:4–5).

The Self also sends its own "storms" upon the ego when the latter chooses to turn its back on the Shadow. The Self seems to recognize that this process of self-division is inherently destructive, and therefore evil, so it sends a variety of psychological disturbances upon the ego in order to push it towards reconciliation with the Shadow.[7] These psychological disturbances can be very stormy indeed, for not only can they generate a prodigious amount of spiritual suffering in the mind, they can also become magnified to the point of catastrophe through the classic pattern of a vicious cycle. The cycle begins when the internally divided individual begins to consciously suffer from his psychospiritual malady. This suffering directly leads to all sorts of convoluted emotions and irrational thinking patterns, which in turn lead to varying degrees of self-destructive behavior in a person's life. These destructive behaviors then generate even more pain and turmoil within the soul, which in turn lead to still more destructive behavior, and so on, until the vicious cycle is either short-circuited by some type of heroic intervention or the individual himself is ultimately destroyed.

Jonah and the Unconscious

This is undoubtedly why Jonah has so many brushes with death in his flight away from God's command: because anyone who consistently turns his back on the inner callings of the Self runs the risk of complete self-destruction. One simply cannot expect to be able to divide one's innermost spirit in two for the sake of one's own hedonistic convenience and then expect not to pay dearly for it, even if this self-division happens primarily on an unconscious level. The Bible reiterates this important message by teaching that God is not mocked (Gal. 6:7); as a result of this, we cannot expect to be able to flaunt His spiritual laws without severe consequences resulting. After all, the human personality was originally designed to be a single integrated unit (at least in its final self-actualized form), so it can only be expected to function properly in this unified capacity. It stands to reason, then, that when we unconsciously try to break up this primordial wholeness for our own selfish convenience, the very forces of hell will naturally be called out to punish us.

It is important to note, however, that this punishment doesn't appear to be meted out by an external being. It is, rather, something that happens of its own accord within us when certain psychospiritual laws within the mind are transgressed. In effect, then, we end up punishing ourselves through natural cause and effect means when we behave inappropriately, and this process of self-punishment tends to continue until the underlying psychological problem is eventually corrected.

The story line of Jonah follows this basic train of thought through to the letter, insofar as it tells us that the storm was directly caused by Jonah, through his explicit refusal to follow the Lord's command. This is symbolic of how we tend to punish ourselves through natural causal means whenever we try to run away from the direction of the inner Self. The book of Jonah symbolizes this process of self-punishment by pointing out that Jonah's ship was threatening to break apart because of the viciousness of the storm. In fact, the storm was so bad that Jonah's fellow passengers were forced to throw everything they possibly could overboard so they could stay afloat.

The auxiliary forces of the ego, however, will naturally do everything in their power, short of actually facing and reintegrating the Shadow, to make the ego's suffering less aversive, and therefore more tolerable. They will streamline the ego's life in every possible way, and may even cause it to resort to drugs or alcohol to make its suffering more manageable. In the end, though, no amount of streamlining or painkilling can ever placate the angry Self, because the only thing that the Self will settle for is a reunion between the ego and its Shadow, no matter how unpleasant it may happen to be, because this is the only way our species-based goal of individuation can take place.

The sea is the great symbol of the unconscious *par excellence*. Accordingly, the violence of the sea in the story of Jonah is symbolic of the tremendous amount of anger that tends to be exhibited by the unconscious whenever the ego forces it to conceal an important part of the larger personality. Moreover, just as the sailors on Jonah's ship were unable to quell the storm (or the effects of the storm on the ship itself) by throwing the ship's cargo into the sea, so too is the ego unable to quell the emotional storms of the unconscious through temporary, stop-gap measures.

In many archetypally-based stories the psychic phenomenon of repression tends to be symbolized in the form of a person who is fast asleep. This makes sense, because as far as the repressed contents of the unconscious are concerned, the ego is indeed "asleep." Naturally, then, Jonah turns out to be asleep when the great storm initially strikes:

> But Jonah had gone below deck, where he lay down and fell into a deep sleep. The captain went to him and said, "How can you sleep? Get up and call on your god! Maybe he will take notice of us, and we will not perish" (Jonah 1:5 6).

We are specifically told that Jonah had gone "below deck" in order to sleep. This directly symbolizes the subterranean nature of the repressive process. Amazingly, though, Jonah is able to sleep right through the violent storm, just as the ego is able to go through its entire life not being aware of its own Shadow. The captain of the ship, however, is astonished to learn that Jonah has been asleep during the entire storm, so he wakes Jonah up and urges him to call on his God, so that they might not perish.

The captain of the ship, of course, is yet another symbol of the Self, or more specifically, of that instinctual part of the Self that tells us it is wrong to repress *any* part of our personality. It repeatedly urges us to do whatever we possibly can to make things right within our own souls, just as the captain of the ship urges Jonah to call out to his god as a last-ditch effort to save all their lives.

In characteristically human fashion, though, the ego tends to wait until the last possible moment before it will agree to face the truth of its own inner sickness. This is symbolized in our Biblical story by Jonah's initial choice to do nothing in response to the captain's urgings. This leaves the sailors no alternative but to take matters into their own hands, because Jonah clearly isn't going to take any constructive action until he literally has no other choice. This dramatic development is symbolic of how the paralyzed ego tends to require some sort of external intervention before it will be able to break the deadlock between itself and the repressed Shadow.

> Then the sailors said to each other, "Come, let us cast lots to find out who is responsible for this calamity." They cast lots and the lot fell on Jonah. So they asked him, "Tell us, who is responsible for making all this trouble

for us? What do you do? Where do you come from? What is your country? From what people are you?"

He answered, "I am a Hebrew and I worship the Lord, the God of heaven, who made the sea and the land."

This terrified them and they asked, "What have you done?" (They knew he was running away from the Lord, because he had already told them so.)

The sea was getting rougher and rougher. So they asked him, "What should we do to you to make the sea calm down for us?"

"Pick me up and throw me into the sea," he replied, "and it will become calm. I know that it is my fault that this great storm has come upon you."

Instead, the men did their best to row back to land. But they could not, for the sea grew even wilder than before. Then they cried to the Lord, "O Lord, please do not let us die for taking this man's life. Do not hold us accountable for killing an innocent man, for you, O Lord, have done as you pleased." Then they took Jonah and threw him overboard, and the raging sea grew calm. At this the men greatly feared the Lord, and they offered a sacrifice to the Lord and made vows to him. But the Lord provided a great fish to swallow Jonah, and Jonah was inside the fish three days and three nights.

It is an interesting fact of life that, more often than not, we tend to create "lucky" or "unlucky" situations for ourselves, depending on how we choose to behave in the world. If we behave in a manner that is consistent with the Self's inner developmental demands, we will tend to create "lucky" situations for ourselves, and conversely, if we behave in a manner that thwarts the inner demands of the Self, we will tend to create "unlucky" situations for ourselves. The casting of lots on the ship is thus symbolic of the intimate relationship that typically exists between "luck" and our just due in life. This being the case, it is no wonder that the lot falls upon Jonah: since he is guilty, he *can't help* but behave in a way that seems to make the "luck of the draw" work against him.

The sailors became terrified when they learned that Jonah was running away from the Lord. This is analogous to the fear that the superego, or conscience, feels when it discovers that we have been running away from an important part of ourselves for an entire lifetime. This fear and self-loathing is entirely appropriate, though, because the real-world implications of a split personality are truly monumental, as we have seen. We simply cannot repress away a major part of our personality without incurring the full wrath of the Self, and the superego knows that.

The fact that the sea continued to get rougher and rougher, even though the true cause of the problem (Jonah) had already been found, is highly significant, because it means that simple awareness of the problem of repression will never be sufficient to make things OK in and of itself. Heroic action is what is required, and this is symbolized in the story by the fact that Jonah had to literally be thrown overboard before the sea would calm down.

Interestingly enough, Jonah turns out to be fully aware of the storm's true cause. Now, one might initially think that this would have never been the case, but this isn't true at all. To the contrary, Jonah's high degree of personal awareness is symbolic of how the Self (and sometimes even the ego) tends to know deep down why it is suffering so intensely. In spite of this inner awareness, though, the ego tends to persist in its maladaptive behavior until the last possible moment, because it needs to experience a truly monumental amount of suffering before it can be driven to the point that it can take a spontaneous leap into the great unknown. This in itself provides a powerful justification for the existence of evil in the world, for without pain and suffering to prod the ego beyond its pathological boundaries, it would probably remain imprisoned within these boundaries forever. John Sanford agrees:

> So reluctant are men to see themselves as they really are and to face their inner contradiction that it is only by the greatest of efforts that most people can be brought to this self-confrontation. The vast majority prefer the wide way of unconsciousness which leads to ignorance of the inner enemy. This is destructive, because ignorance of the inner enemy by no means resolves the problem. To the contrary, the enemy now appears in the guise of other people, and the hostility which has its origin in ourselves takes the form of hostility to others.[8]

The ego has good reason to drag its feet when it comes to effecting its own liberation from these self-imposed boundaries: it is much easier and less painful in the short-term to remain in a pathological state of mind than it is to face the truth of one's inner contradiction and to attempt to break out of it. Indeed, Jonah was probably caught up in this ethic of non-action as well; that is, until the storm got so bad that something *had* to be done about it.

Even so, the sailors did everything they could to row back to land, but to no avail, because the sea continued to get wilder and wilder with each passing moment. This, as we have seen, is symbolic of how the ego will typically try every stop-gap procedure in the book before it will finally give in and face its own Shadow.

Before the sailors actually threw Jonah into the sea, however, they prayed to God that they would not be held accountable for the killing of an innocent life. This is symbolic of how the ego will typically issue a last-ditch appeal for help and forgiveness as it prepares to face its own Shadow. Indeed, the very foreboding that it generated by this risky action makes such a calling out almost inevitable.

In a similar vein, Jonah's last-minute decision to allow himself to be thrown into the sea is symbolic of the ego's decision, under duress, to face the contents of its own unconscious, no matter how aversive they may happen to be. *Thus, Jonah's actual entry into the sea is symbolic of the ego's unilateral choice to submerge itself within the Shadow's own unconscious contents.*

One of the most significant features of this Biblical drama is the response of the sea to Jonah's behavior. Before he is thrown in, the sea is wild and deadly, but just as soon as Jonah takes his fateful plunge, it suddenly becomes quiet and placid. This is directly symbolic of how the Self's extreme wrath tends to immediately be placated just as soon as the ego decides to "jump in" and face the dreaded Shadow. For not only does the Self's demand for wholeness get partially satisfied by this sort of integrative behavior, the Shadow's own unruly effect on the mind also tends to get quelled by it as well.

Indeed, psychologist Arthur Janov has taken great pains to show that it isn't our unconscious pains in and of themselves that cause us the most discomfort when we split ourselves off from them; it is, rather, our militant *opposition* to them that causes us by far the greatest agony. Hence, once we decide to give in to our unconscious leanings, much of our inner pain will instantly dissipate, just as the sea instantly quieted down the moment Jonah was thrown into it.

It is important to remember that Jonah didn't voluntarily choose to jump into the sea, even though he knew that he had to do so before the storm would calm down. Rather, he insisted on being thrown overboard by the sailors themselves. This is symbolic of the fact that the ego's descent into the unconscious is rarely, if ever, a free, uncompelled choice. To the contrary, it is almost always a "choice" that is inadvertently forced upon the ego by its stubborn refusal to face its own Shadow, which in turn causes it to suffer an extreme amount of inner pain and turmoil. It is this pain that compels the ego to undertake this most undesirable of tasks. This is why the arrival of the kingdom of God in an individual is almost always heralded by a profound degree of pain and suffering: because it is this inner discomfort that compels the ego to make peace with the Shadow, and it is the resulting psychospiritual wholeness that enables one to automatically enter the kingdom.

The actual process of entering the kingdom, however, doesn't appear to be directly mediated by an external being, as popular opinion holds; rather, it appears to be a process that is largely mediated by the individual's *own* level of conscious awareness. On this view, the actualized personality will naturally be catapulted into a direct personal experience of the kingdom by its own transcendent level of conscious awareness.

A useful analogy can be drawn here to the process of radio broadcasting. It is a well-known fact that many different radio signals pass through the air at any given time, yet none of them can actually be perceived until a radio receiver is tuned to a certain occupied frequency. Thus, while a given radio station may be broadcasting at a frequency of 102.5 megahertz 24 hours a day, the programming itself can only be perceived when a radio receiver is actually tuned to 102.5.

In the same way, we can say that the kingdom of God also exists at all times as a distinct spiritual potentiality within us, yet it cannot be directly experienced until we first "tune" ourselves to the right spiritual "frequency" by becoming fully individuated, for the more mature and developed we become, the more we will be able to naturally perceive the spiritual world around us and within us. Once again we see that it is the process of spiritual growth that is the *sine qua non* of our religious mission on this planet.

This developmental interpretation of the kingdom is strongly supported by Jesus' contention that the kingdom of God isn't as much a physical place as it is an internal state of mind, as the following quote well illustrates:

> Once, having been asked by the Pharisees when the kingdom of God would come, Jesus replied, "The kingdom of God does not come with your careful observation, nor will people say, 'Here it is,' or 'There it is,' *because the kingdom of God is within you*" (Luke 17:21, emphasis mine).

Now, if the kingdom of God is truly within us, then it is easy to see how an ambitious process of self-development can put us into direct touch with our Maker. This is doubly true if God is postulated to exist in the innermost part of the soul, because in this case it is possible for the mind's many repressions to completely block our free and direct access to our inner spiritual depths, which is where the God within us presumably exists. On the other hand, if we can dismantle our mind's repressions, and thereby clear the way to God's residing place deep within the soul, it then becomes easy to see how an inner process of soul-cleansing can be capable of initiating us into the kingdom.

Significance of the Fish

Another tantalizing part of the story of Jonah concerns God's use of a "great fish" to save Jonah's life once he is thrown into the raging sea. We are further told that Jonah remained inside the fish for three days and three nights.[9]

Metaphorically speaking, a fish symbolizes a person who can survive and even thrive in the "undersea" realm of the unconscious for prolonged periods of time. Perhaps this is why the fish was such a potent symbol in Christianity's early years: because the first Christians were primarily interested in navigating through the inner realm of the spirit—which is what we call the unconscious today—so they could purify themselves of their accumulated evils and thereby find God within their own souls.

It isn't surprising, then, that a great fish provides a safe haven for Jonah, in the midst of an extremely dangerous set of personal circumstances. This of course is symbolic of how the Lord will also provide a safe haven for the ego once it decides to immerse itself within the "raging seas" of the unconscious. Elsewhere the Bible states this same reality once again: the Lord will not allow us to be "tempted" beyond that which we are able to withstand (1 Cor. 10:13), and this seems to apply just as much to intrapsychic events as it does to events in the outside world.

The existence of this safe haven is particularly important for us today, because it means that we needn't be afraid of this required descent into our unconscious. For no matter how dangerous such a descent might superficially appear to be, God (or the natural order, which in this case amounts to the same thing) will ultimately provide a safe haven for us to survive in.

The fact that Jonah remained inside the fish for three days and three nights is also significant, because it means that the work we need to do inside the unconscious is not instantaneous. To the contrary, this inner work tends to involve a long and drawn-out process that is as emotionally taxing as it is time-consuming, due to the large number of repressed pains that have typically been accumulated within the unconscious by the time we become adults. But no matter how difficult it is or how much time it takes, we can rest assured knowing that God has promised to protect us from harm while we are reclaiming the lost parts of our personality.

The Prayer

Moving on with our story, the Bible tells us that Jonah prayed an elaborate prayer to the Lord while he was confined inside the great fish:

> He said: "In my distress I called to the Lord, and he answered me. From the depths of the grave I called for help, and you listened to my cry. You hurled me into the deep, into the very heart of the seas, and the currents swirled about me; all your waves and breakers swept over me. I said, 'I have been banished from your sight; yet I will look again toward your holy temple.'
>
> "The engulfing waters threatened me, the deep surrounded me; seaweed was wrapped around my head. To the roots of the mountains I sank down; the earth beneath barred me in forever. But you brought my life up from the pit, O Lord my God.
>
> "When my life was ebbing away, I remembered you, Lord, and my prayer rose to you, to your holy temple. Those who cling to worthless idols forfeit the grace that could be theirs. But I, with a song of thanksgiving, will

sacrifice to you. What I have vowed I will make good. Salvation comes from the Lord" (Jonah 2:2-9).

This is a very interesting prayer that makes our psychological interpretation of the book of Jonah almost unmistakable. For Jonah openly admits that he has been in a profound state of distress. Even more significantly, he also says that he has been thrown "into the deep, into the very heart of the seas." Not coincidentally, these are some of the most common psychological terms that are used today to describe the unconscious, especially in poetic literature. Jonah further points out that the currents of the sea swirled about him, and that the "engulfing waters" threatened him. These are clear references to the emotional beating that one typically takes when the wrath of the unconscious suddenly becomes unleashed. Indeed, people commonly report that they feel like they're dying when they suddenly take the plunge into their own inner depths. And in fact, Jonah claims to have called for help from within the "depths of the grave," just as he further states that his life was "ebbing away" during his outrageous ordeal.

It is precisely at this point, however, that the person who is seriously intent on reaching wholeness must persevere through the immediate pains and fears of the journey. While the inner demons of the unconscious may indeed be intimidating, one must nevertheless look beyond them to the great Creator Himself for the strength to carry on, as Kierkegaard originally pointed out with his suggestion that we take a "leap of faith" beyond our fears to the eternal security of the Godhead. On Kierkegaard's view, there is no doubt that God will hear us and grant us the strength to persevere if we sincerely call upon Him during our time of innermost longing.

It isn't necessary, though, to posit a bona fide miracle here to account for the appearance of this newfound inner strength. It is also possible that the human mind has been set up all along to naturalistically respond in this fashion when the name of God is sincerely called upon, and indeed, the very act of looking upward for strength seems to coax it out of the innermost recesses of our souls. But even if this is so, it doesn't necessarily negate the objective validity of our faith in God. It merely means that our religious faith can be objectively true *via* the natural cause and effect principles that have been built into us from the very beginning. After all, why should God perform an external miracle to cleanse us when we can achieve the same effect naturalistically by sincerely calling upon His name?

This is precisely what Jonah did in the midst of his suffering inside the great fish. In fact, Jonah went so far as to totally recommit himself to his Maker during this time of reconciliation, and this had the beneficial effect of appeasing the Lord, which in turn caused Him to command the fish to regurgitate Jonah back onto dry land:

And the Lord commanded the fish, and it vomited Jonah onto dry land (Jonah 2:10).

In other words, it was Jonah's humility, *vis-à-vis* the Lord and his own inner development, that was the chief motivating factor that drove God to free Jonah from the horrible insides of the great fish. Interestingly enough, this same principle can be shown to apply to the process of psychospiritual development as well, for the only way we can re-emerge in one piece from our inner neurotic suffering is if we first develop enough meekness of heart to allow us to become reconciled with the Shadow side of our personalities. Once this meekness presents itself, the remainder of the conciliatory process becomes relatively easy, because we must first become meek *before* we can reintegrate the Shadow within the mainstream of our personality. This is why the fish spits Jonah out just as soon as the latter becomes right spiritually: because it is the development of the right spiritual attitude that is the crucial limiting factor in any process of psychospiritual reconciliation. Once this critical bottleneck is overcome, everything else is more or less "downhill," including our relationship with the Lord. This is due to the fact that the same principles that mediate our own inner development also mediate our relationship with our Creator, whether we are consciously aware of it or not.[10]

It should come as no surprise, then, that the psychospiritual trait of humility is intimately related to the quality of our personal relationship (or lack of one) with God. After all, we can't even *begin* to become aware of God as the spiritual Center of our lives until we first become humble, because our personal pride almost always stands in the way. A similar principle also applies to our acknowledgment of God's existence in the universe: we can't "confess" God in this manner until we first become humble inside, because personal pride greatly constricts our capacity to draw accurate and rational conclusions about the true nature of reality.

The Mission to Nineveh

Getting back to our story, we find that once the fish vomited Jonah back out onto dry land, the Lord spoke to him a second time:

Then the word of the Lord came to Jonah a second time: "Go to the great city of Nineveh and proclaim to it the message I give you."

Jonah obeyed the word of the Lord and went to Nineveh. Now Nineveh was a very important city—a visit required three days.

On the first day, Jonah started into the city. He proclaimed: "Forty more days and Nineveh will be overturned."

The Ninevites believed God. They declared a fast, and all of them, from the greatest to the least, put on sackcloth. When the news reached the king of Nineveh, he rose from his throne, took off his royal robes, covered himself with sackcloth and sat down in the dust. Then he issued a proclamation in Nineveh:

"By the decree of the king and his nobles: Do not let any man or beast, herd or flock, taste anything; do not let them eat or drink. But let man and beast be covered with sackcloth. Let everyone call urgently on God. Let them give up their evil ways and their violence. Who knows? God may yet relent and with compassion turn from his fierce anger so that we will not perish."

When God saw what they did and how they turned from their evil ways, he had compassion and did not bring upon them the destruction he had threatened (Jonah 3:1-10).

In this highly revealing passage, the author emphasizes the fact that Nineveh was a "very important city." Indeed, it was so great that it required a lengthy visit of three days just to see it all. This is a highly suggestive statement from a metaphorical point of view, because as we have seen, the city of Nineveh symbolically represents the unconscious part of the mind. Hence, the author is actually telling us that the unconscious is so important that it takes three solid "days" just to see it all. This is symbolic of the fact that our reconciliation with the Shadow is invariably a time-consuming process, as we have seen. We simply cannot reintegrate back into consciousness a lifetime of repressed pains and fears overnight.

It is significant to note that Jonah's actual preaching to the city isn't described in negative terms at all. It is, to the contrary, Jonah's *avoidance* of this important task that causes him to experience so much pain and heartache. Again we find that the same principle applies without exception to our inner course of development—it isn't the act of facing the Shadow that causes us to consciously suffer; it is, rather, the neurotic *avoidance* of the Shadow that causes us to experience untold amounts of grief.

This phenomenon has been described in very precise clinical terms by Los Angeles psychologist Arthur Janov, creator of Primal Therapy. Janov has repeatedly noted that it isn't the actual facing of one's repressed feelings that is subjectively experienced as painful. It is, rather, our pathological *defense* against these repressions that causes us to agonize so profoundly. Indeed, this inner transition between painful self-defense and emotional relief—which is said to be simultaneous with the actual immersion of the individual into his or her past pain—has repeatedly been described as being highly dramatic and *very* fulfilling, especially over the long term.

It is important to note here that the word of the Lord, which is analogous to the callings of the inner Self in Jung's analytic psychology, came to Jonah on a second occasion, after he had been forcefully ejected from the belly of the great fish. This represents the Self's second attempt to motivate the ego into making peace with the Shadow. Fortunately, Jonah had fully prepared himself to heed the Lord's command this second time around, since he had suffered more than enough to eliminate his former fear and hubris. In the same fashion, the ego is also better able to heed the inner demands of the Self after it has suffered a great deal, because nothing is able to defuse pride and fear better than pain.

We have seen how the wickedness of the Ninevites is directly symbolic of the pain and suffering that is routinely produced by the Shadow when the ego fails to include it within the overall matrix of the personality. We mustn't forget, however, that the wickedness of the Shadow is not an intrinsic feature of these repressions *per se*. It is merely an intrinsic feature of the ego's process of denial.

That is to say, as long as the ego persists in keeping the Shadow repressed, these repressed elements will continue to fight back by producing a great deal of wickedness. However, as soon as the ego waves the white flag, so to speak, and makes a genuine peace offering to the Shadow, the latter's former wickedness will quickly disappear. This psychic phenomenon is symbolized in the Biblical story of Jonah by the extreme cooperativeness of the Ninevites with the Lord's command for repentance. They didn't hesitate to reform themselves once Jonah delivered his initial warning, and neither will our Shadow hesitate to change for the better once we finally decide to reincorporate it within our personalities. And, of course, once the Self "sees" that the Shadow has been transformed and reintegrated within the personality, it will simultaneously relax its previous threat to destroy the personality. This is symbolized in the story by God's compassion on the city of Nineveh and by His decision to give it a second chance.[11]

Now, you'd think that Jonah would have been ecstatic knowing that he had saved an entire city through his noble actions as a prophet. Remarkably, though, Jonah became very angry with God when he discovered that God had decided to spare the lives of the Ninevites because of their city-wide act of repentance:

> When God saw what they [the Ninevites] did and how they turned from their evil ways, he had compassion and did not bring upon them the destruction he had threatened.
>
> But Jonah was greatly displeased and became angry. He prayed to the Lord, "O Lord, is this not what I said when I was still at home? that is why I was so quick to flee to Tarshish. I knew that you are a gracious and compassionate God, slow to anger and abounding in love, a God who relents from sending calamity. Now, O Lord, take away my life, for it is better for me to die than to live" (Jonah 3:10; 4:1–3).

Jonah became angry for two reasons. First, as a Hebrew, Jonah would have preferred to see Nineveh destroyed altogether, since the Ninevites were the enemies of Israel.[12]

Secondly, Jonah was apparently afflicted with the sin of laziness, so he became angry when he saw that he had to go through such a tremendous ordeal in order to save the city of Nineveh, when God was apparently planning to spare it all along. This response is somewhat understandable (at least for Jonah), because few people would ever want to go through such an outrageous sequence of events in order to contribute to the occurrence of something that was presumably going to happen anyway.

On a superficial level, Jonah's mistake was to assume that God would have spared the city of Nineveh, whether or not he would have actually preached to the city. Of course, this is something that Jonah couldn't possibly have known, because the Mind of God is truly unsearchable in this capacity.

Jonah apparently didn't realize that it was his own behavior that made the crucial difference between Nineveh being destroyed and its being saved. Although Jonah was correct in believing that God would have been just as kind and slow-to-anger had he not preached to the Ninevites, he was wrong to believe that God would have spared the Ninevites in either case. For it was the behavior of the Ninevites themselves that made the crucial difference in whether or not the city was actually going to be destroyed, and *not* the lovingkindness of God *per se*.

As we just saw in an earlier footnote, when the Bible speaks of God sparing or condemning a city in the Old Testament, it doesn't necessarily mean a unilateral act on the part of God Himself. More often than not, it seems to refer to a unilateral act on the part of *humans*, and not God, in the sense that *they* are the ones who are either making or breaking their chance for survival with their own behavior. For the sake of simplicity, though, the Bible often chooses to refer to this process of self-destruction as something the Lord brings about, when in reality it is something that humans themselves are actually responsible for; God simply makes the world function in such a way that humans can bring about any number of different consequences with their behavior.

Jonah also showed his overall lack of maturity when he became angry with God for sparing the enemies of Israel. Had Jonah possessed a more mature understanding of his Creator, he would have realized that God doesn't save or condemn whole cities of people on the basis of world-based political factors alone. As far as God is concerned, *all* people deserve a chance to be spared from His wrath if they choose to turn from their evil ways, even if they happen to be the enemies of Israel. Indeed, one of the evils that the Ninevites could very well have repented of is their political opposition to the state of Israel.

Needless to say, God wasn't happy with Jonah's anger, or with his irresponsible request for death instead of life. He even tells Jonah that he has no right at all to be angry for what has happened (Jonah 4:4).

In response to this Divine rebuff, Jonah removed himself to the outskirts of the city, where he:

> . . . made himself a shelter, sat in its shade and waited to see what would happen to the city. Then the Lord God provided a vine and made it grow up over Jonah to give shade for his head to ease his discomfort, and Jonah was very happy about the vine. But at dawn the next day God provided a worm, which chewed the vine so that it withered. When the sun rose, God provided a scorching east wind, and the sun blazed on Jonah's head so that he grew faint. He wanted to die, and said, "It would be better for me to die than to live."
>
> But God said to Jonah, "Do you have a right to be angry about the vine?"
>
> "I do," he said. "I am angry enough to die."
>
> But the Lord said, "You have been concerned about this vine, though you did not tend it or make it grow. It sprang up overnight and died overnight. But Nineveh has more than a hundred and twenty thousand people who cannot tell their right hand from their left, and many cattle as well. Should I not be concerned about that great city" (Jonah 4:5–11)?

We can see from the above passage that the Lord utilized a natural feature of the earth to teach Jonah about the virtue of compassion. Although the Bible tells us that God directly caused the vine to grow over Jonah's head, and that He caused the worm to eat the vine, this once again could be a literary reference to an entirely natural process that God simply took advantage of to teach Jonah an important lesson.

God's point is that Jonah came to love and appreciate the vine even though it sprang up overnight, and even though he had nothing to do with its arrival. Similarly, Jonah quickly came to hate the worm that destroyed the vine on the following day, because without the vine he no longer had any shade to comfort himself with.

In His infinite wisdom, though, the Lord then asks Jonah whether or not he has a right to be angry about the vine, and of course, Jonah answers in the affirmative. But then the Lord points out to Jonah that the great city of Nineveh is far more valuable than a mere vine, so if Jonah is going to be upset about the loss of "his" vine, then he should also be that much *more* upset about the possible loss of an entire city of people. God even adds a subtle bit of sarcasm to His reply to Jonah, because He points out that there were also many cattle in the city as well, which Jonah wouldn't have wanted to see perish, either. The basic idea here is that if Jonah is unable to appreciate what it would mean to lose an entire city of people, then surely he must be able to appreciate what it would mean to lose so many precious animals!

God also shows Himself to be aware of human folly and ignorance in His final statement to Jonah, since He tells Jonah that the Ninevites are "more than a hundred and twenty thousand people who cannot tell their right hand from their left. . . . " No one enjoys killing ignorant (and therefore, to some extent, innocent) people when they don't have to, and this apparently includes God as well as humans.

A Theodicy for Natural Evils

We can see in the above lesson about the worm and the vine a valuable function for many of the physical evils in the world. For in this particular case God clearly used the "evil" of the worm to teach Jonah an important lesson about the importance of human life in the Divine Scheme of Things. While the worm might have a caused the loss of an important vine from a short-term point of view, from a larger viewpoint it caused Jonah to learn something important about life. The paradigm here is that of God's using the physical destructiveness of the world to teach immature human beings important spiritual lessons about the meaning of life.

As many other authors have pointed out, there is good reason for supposing that this is a viable justification for many of the natural evils of this world.[13] In support of this conclusion, it cannot be denied that the existence of physical evil in the world has been a great promoter of character over the millennia, just as it has also taught billions of important lessons to people throughout history.

On the negative side, though, critics have charged that there is too much natural evil in the world to be consistent with the existence of a good and omnipotent Creator, especially with respect to natural catastrophes such as earthquakes and hurricanes. While many important lessons may in fact be learned from such catastrophes, critics argue that these lessons are more than outweighed by the sheer waste and destructiveness that is caused by them. Take the great Lisbon earthquake of 1755 for instance. While it undoubtedly taught thousands of people many important lessons, it also caused tens of thousands of innocent men, women, and children to lose their lives in one tremendous upheaval. How could these innocent victims have possibly learned anything constructive from this unfortunate tragedy?

This is a good criticism of the orthodox theistic position, and from a certain limited point of view it seems to make good sense. However, from a long-term viewpoint that includes the existence of an Afterlife it becomes far less convincing, because the Afterlife *itself* can help to right many of the wrongs that were done to people in this lifetime. Moreover, if it is acknowledged that some degree of natural evil is necessary if we are to have a stable environment of physical laws in which free behaviors can take place, then we see that the reality of natural evil doesn't itself necessarily preclude the existence of a justifiable reason for this evil. This conclusion is further buttressed by the fact that there are a great many pathological conditions of the human spirit that are so extreme that they are generally unaffected by all but the most extreme of natural disasters.

These internal blockages are exceedingly evil, insofar as they stultify the developmental progress of the individual as long as they continue to exist. They are also incomparably tenacious as well, insofar as nothing less than the most heroic of efforts will typically succeed in vanquishing them. The almost complete intractability of the depraved human spirit was well recognized by Albert Einstein, who once wrote that "it is easier to denature plutonium than it is to denature the evil spirit of man."

The upshot of this realization is that our minds are far more possessed by various pathological syndromes than most of us have ever previously realized. Indeed, this possession is so complete that many people *don't even recognize* that they are possessed by any evil tendencies in the first place, but of course, the very worst kinds of evil are those which masquerade themselves as good in the mind.

Now, if our explicit purpose in this lifetime is to grow to be as mature and developed as possible, as many progressive thinkers from Jesus to Jung have independently concluded, it is clear that we need to get rid of these internal developmental barriers at the earliest possible moment, because as long as they continue to exist, the ultimate purpose of God on this planet will never be achieved. It follows from this conclusion that the Divine purpose requires the existence of some form of natural power in the world that can effectively penetrate, and subsequently annihilate, these internal barriers once and for all. But if these developmental barriers are as rigid and sinister as we have postulated them to be, then the only way they are ever going to be overcome is through the occurrence of many truly horrific natural evils; anything less will simply not be sufficient to budge them from their demonic possession of the human spirit.

While these catastrophic evils must inevitably end up killing and maiming large numbers of people from time to time (otherwise they wouldn't be sufficiently catastrophic), this is only an insurmountable theological problem as long as we deny the existence of an additional world beyond the grave where we can continue the process of development that we began in this world. If, on the other hand, we postulate the existence of an Afterlife (as most of the world's major religions have done), then those individuals who end up being inadvertently killed in the natural disasters of this world will nevertheless be able to continue living and growing in the next world, where they will then be able to use the developmental lessons that they learned from their untimely demise to help them overcome their remaining impediments to growth. And, as far as the survivors of these natural catastrophes are concerned, they can begin implementing their newly acquired growth-facilitating powers right away in this world.

In fact, as long as we affirm the ultimate value of the human developmental process in the Cosmic Scheme of Things, and as long as we affirm the existence of pathological barriers in the mind that naturally act to thwart this development, it follows that it is better in the long run for a person to die in a natural disaster, and to thereby get rid of these internal barriers to growth (assuming that this is indeed what happens), than it is for a person to survive in this world with these evil barriers intact. The point is simply that we *can* reconcile the existence of catastrophic evil in this world with the existence of a good and omnipotent God, but *only* if we maintain a realistic appreciation for the true depth of human wickedness, as well as for the truly heroic means that must be used to overcome it. This is, in fact, the ultimate meaning of the cross in human life: we need to die, not just spiritually, but oftentimes physically as well, in order to be able to overcome our many psychological barriers to growth, so we can then be reborn into a higher state of spiritual awareness.

It would appear, then, that we have grossly underestimated both the strength of our many inner impediments to growth, as well as the degree of personal response that is necessary to overcome them. We aren't talking here about a few leisurely hangups that are of little ultimate importance to our overall process of development. Rather, we are talking about an all-encompassing, systemic *possession* of our innermost soul by a wicked and neurotic system that is hell-bent on blocking our growth *forevermore*; that is, until it can be successfully uprooted from our system once and for all. Unfortunately, this inner evil can't be pacified, attenuated, or negotiated with; it can only be destroyed through heroic (and sometimes even violent) means. This is why our world of extreme evil is teleologically necessary in the larger Scheme of Things: because nothing less than an utterly catastrophic personal experience will typically suffice to eliminate these inner developmental barriers once and for all, so that we can continue our process of growth towards our long-term goal of individuation.

Interestingly enough, the literal translation of the word "satan" in the Old Testament fits in very well with this developmental paradigm, insofar as it literally means an "obstacle or adversary that impedes our free forward movement." The "obstacle" or "adversary" in this case can simply be thought of as a reference to *any* type of psychopathology that is capable of impeding our free forward movement towards our own self-actualization. We can therefore think of these inner developmental barriers as true psychological "satans" who are intent on stultifying our free forward movement towards individuation forever.

Indeed, the entire concept of demon possession, as we have seen, also fits very nicely within this developmental scheme, because as long as there are any significant neurotic barriers within the mind, they will end up "possessing" our souls and minds in an absolute sense, determining who we are, what we think, and how we feel, *indefinitely*. Worst of all, they will also continue to function like a psychospiritual "straightjacket" within the larger personality, withholding happiness from us in the present and blocking our free forward movement towards our own individuation. No wonder Jesus likened these developmental barriers to true demonic possession, because they *really do* possess our souls in a negative fashion, ruining our lives for as long as they continue to exist.

It is in this sense that it becomes necessary to "fight fire with fire" in the larger personality structure itself, because by far the most effective way of defusing these inner evils is through some type of personal experience with extreme suffering. This suffering can either be elicited by an external evil event or through an internal amplification of psychic pain. In either case, though, it is possible to reach a significant cathartic experience through our own sincere suffering.

It is, of course, our inner state of psychospiritual development that determines how we respond to the various inner and outer events in our lives. As a consequence, if we are sick and divided on the inside, we will probably be unable to mount an adequate response to a wide range of different stressors, and this, in turn, will eventually predispose us towards some type of emotional breakdown as a result. On the other hand, if we have resolved the majority of our inner problems, and thereby have placed ourselves on the right road to spiritual recovery, we will then tend to respond to these stressors by growing stronger and more mature overall. This variable dynamic explains one of Jesus' most enigmatic sayings in the Gospel of Thomas:

> A grapevine has been planted away from the father. Since it is not strong, it will be pulled up by its root and will perish. . . . Whoever has something in hand will be given more, and whoever has nothing will be deprived of even the little that person has (vv. 40–41).

A similar saying can be found in the Gospel of Luke:

> To everyone who has, more will be given, but as for the one who has nothing, even what he has will be taken away (Luke 19:26).

In other words, if we are fortunate enough to have a healthy developmental state "in hand," we will tend to grow progressively more mature with the passage of time, because we will no longer have to do a complete "about-face" in our lives in order to get back on the right developmental road. On the other hand, if we haven't yet gotten on the right road to spiritual recovery, we will eventually have to do a 180 degree turn in our lives before we will be able to start to change for the better. Unfortunately, it is in the very nature of these developmental about-faces that we typically have to suffer a great deal before they will actually happen. This is why Jesus tells us in the above passage that whoever has nothing (in terms of a healthy mental state) will be deprived of even the little that he or she has: because we typically have to lose just about everything before we will agree to repent and change for the better. Indeed, this is the literal meaning of the word "repent" *(metanoia)* in the original Greek: to do a complete about-face in one's life, so that one can begin moving in the opposite direction. This is also where the teleological purpose of suffering comes into play in our lives, for by whittling us down to nothing when we are sick and possessed by pathological forces on the inside, these evils will eventually humble us into doing a complete about-face in our lives, when no such change probably would have ever taken place otherwise.

This is a valid retort to the criticism that the majority of physical evils result in abject human despair, and *not* psychospiritual growth. According to the theist, this negative response to evil is only true in the short-term. In the long-term, however, it is generally believed that people will eventually be able to grow more mature because of their suffering, even if this growth has to take place in the Afterlife. Indeed, since this kind of self-abasement and despair is assumed to be an essential prerequisite for a genuine process of spiritual rebirth, the theist can incorporate the very worst natural evils into the overall matrix of a sufficiently broad developmental process, in which this kind of despair is simply viewed as an essential means to a future psychospiritual flowering.

Of course, this assertion begs the deeper question of why people couldn't have initially been created fully developed to begin with. This alleged possibility, as J.L. Mackie and Antony Flew have pointed out, would have done away with the vast majority of moral evils in our world in one fell swoop, so it understandably constitutes the crux of the theodicy problem for the philosophical theist. Nevertheless, it *can* be effectively answered by arguing that genuine humans necessarily require a gradual process of self-attained development in order to be fully human. This requires us to postulate that the developmental process *itself* is an essential property of the Human Definition, but this isn't as unlikely a premise as it may initially seem, because the only other possibility, that of humans being created ready-made, would have necessitated their epistemological preprogramming from the very beginning, and this clearly would have resulted in the production of automated robots, and *not* genuine humans, who must possess a certain amount of freedom and self-determination in order to be fully human. This is why we can coherently postulate that the developmental process itself must be an essential property of the Human Definition: because it is the logically necessary precondition for a free and self-determining being (since it is not possible for a person to freely determine the course and content of his or her life if it has already been unilaterally determined by God).

Notes

1. Unless otherwise noted, the scriptural quotations in this book will be from the New International Version of the Bible.
2. Meyer, Marvin, transl. *The Gospel of Thomas* (San Francisco: HarperCollins, 1992).
3. Ibid.
4. John A. Sanford, *The Kingdom Within* (San Francisco: Harper & Row, 1987), p. 143.
5. Ernest Becker, *The Denial of Death* (New York: The Free Press, 1973), pp. 47–67, 72–73.
6. In one sense, of course, we will never be able to reach *full* character development, even throughout eternity, because the process of character growth seems to be inherently open-ended by its very nature. Hence, we will probably keep on growing in some sense for as long as we are alive. Nevertheless, we can still attain a degree of character development that is *relatively* complete. In this state of relative completion, we are developed to the point that we can finally perform our intended function in the universe without constantly being prone to behavioral malfunctioning.
7. This reconciliation is necessary because most moral evils can ultimately be traced to the various psychopathologies that are known to be caused by the neurotic process.
8. John A. Sanford, *The Kingdom Within*, pp. 83–84.
9. It is no accident that a fish comprises a major part of this highly symbolic Old Testament story. Fish, of course, were very important spiritual symbols for the early Church Fathers. Jesus and His disciples were fishermen, and Jesus chose to feed the five thousand with a few fish. Not coincidentally, the first food Jesus ate after the Resurrection was also fish. The early Christians even used the shape of a fish as a cryptic symbol for their belief in Christ, probably because of its rich psychological content.
10. Indeed, there are undoubtedly people who have been able to achieve the "right" spiritual attitude, and yet who haven't been able to recognize that they have inadvertently become right with the Lord. However, as far as their own thoughts, feelings, and actions are concerned, they have indeed become right with God, whether they actually know it yet or not.
11. It should be remembered that whenever God threatens to destroy a city in the Bible, it doesn't necessarily refer to an external act of destruction *per se*. This sort of language can also refer to a city that is being destroyed by its own inhabitants. However, since it is God's omnipresent and omnipotent power that allegedly ties all humanly-inspired efficient causes to their corresponding logical effects in the world, as the ancient Stoics believed, it is possible for both God and humans to destroy a city *collectively*: we humans are the ones who initiate the efficient causes that lead to the destruction, while it is God as Logos who links these destructive causes up with their corresponding logical effects. In this sense, humans are indeed the proximate cause of all humanly-inspired evils in the world, but it is God as Logos who metaphysically enables these evil effects to come into being (in response to the evil behaviors of people).

12. Nineveh still exists today in the Middle East in the infamous state of Iraq. It is very interesting to note that the "Iraqis" (i.e., Ninevites) of that time were enemies of Israel, just as they are today. Some things apparently never change in the world.
13. See Bruce Reichenbach's *Evil and a Good God* or John Hick's *Evil and the God of Love* for more on this important point.

CHAPTER THREE
Job

The book of Job is easily one of the most important pieces of literature in the entire Bible, especially with respect to the problem of evil. It raises all of the classic problems of human existence, and delivers an answer that is both startling and immensely satisfying in the end.

Many great thinkers in the past have wrestled with the philosophical issues raised in the book of Job and have found it necessary to address these topics in their writings. This is precisely what the great Swiss psychiatrist C.G. Jung did with his *Answer to Job*. We will explore Jung's ideas concerning the book of Job at length in the next chapter. First, however, we will concentrate on developing an accurate psychological interpretation of this timeless story.

The Story of Job

The Bible tells us that Job was a very good man before the arrival of his many calamities. In fact, he is said to have been one of the most blameless and admirable people in the entire world at that time:

> In the land of Uz there lived a man whose name was Job. This man was blameless and upright; he feared God and shunned evil. He had seven sons and three daughters, and he owned seven thousand sheep, three thousand camels, five hundred yoke of oxen and five hundred donkeys, and had a large number of servants. He was the greatest man among all the people of the East.
>
> His sons used to take turns holding feasts in their homes, and they would invite their three sisters to eat and drink with them. When a period of feasting had run its course, Job would send and have them purified. Early in the morning he would sacrifice a burnt offering for each of them, thinking, "Perhaps my children have sinned and cursed God in their hearts." This was Job's regular custom (Job 1:1–5).

These initial verses are very deceptive. We are told that Job was the greatest man in all the East, but this doesn't necessarily mean that he was perfect in the eyes of God, or that he was as mature and blameless as it was humanly possible to be at the time. It simply means that compared to the other people of his area, Job was the greatest and most blameless. But this statement clearly has little objective meaning in itself, since it is possible that all the other people in Job's area were sin-filled hedonists. Consequently, the *most* that we can properly conclude from his Biblical description is that compared to everyone else in his area, Job was *relatively* blameless. But this leaves open the possibility that Job was still less than ideally developed before God.

Three factors lend support to this latter interpretation. First, judging from the widespread brutality that existed in Job's time (as it does today in a different form), Job didn't need to be very saintlike in order to be relatively blameless in his violent society. Secondly, Job *couldn't* have been fully individuated at this relatively early point in his development, because this overly ambitious goal is next to impossible to attain in this earthly plane alone. But if this is so, then Job couldn't have been truly blameless before God, at least not on the inside, because the only time God will apparently be satisfied with us is when we become fully self-actualized or individuated, because this is the only way that we can be more or less guaranteed *not* to engage in gratuitous moral evils. Immature individuals don't have enough knowledge or moral fiber by definition to be able to avoid producing destructive consequences with their behavior; hence, the goal of life, at least insofar as the production of moral evil is concerned, must be to become fully grown or individuated. Unfortunately, this developmental goal is so complex and ambitious that almost no one is able to attain it during this lifetime (hence the need for additional worlds beyond the grave where we can continue our ongoing developmental task). But if this is so, then Job almost certainly was *not* fully individuated when his trials began, which means that he *couldn't* have been truly blameless before God (at least not from this objective developmental perspective).

Of course, we're not talking here about being good in an external, behavioral fashion. In this capacity Job was clearly unsurpassed (Job 1: 4–5). However, the Pharisees of Jesus' time were also "good" in this external way, but they were a far cry from being blameless before God. Indeed, genuine spiritual goodness, as John Sanford has pointed out, is *internally* based, because it originates in a clean and blameless inner heart. Consequently, when one's innermost soul has been purified in this manner, one naturally becomes so good on the inside that one can't help but be good on the outside as well, because one's external goodness naturally flows out of the internal goodness of one's state of being. Jesus was keenly aware of this vital spiritual law, as the following quote well illustrates:

> Make a tree good and its fruit will be good, or make a tree bad and its fruit will be bad, for a tree is recognized by its fruit. You brood of vipers, how can you who are evil say anything good? For out of the overflow of

the heart the mouth speaks. The good man brings good things out of the good stored up in him, and the evil man brings evil things out of the evil stored up in him (Matt. 12: 33-37).

However, it is also true that one's outer "goodness" can be feigned in a hypocritical manner. This would be the case if one's outer goodness didn't correspond to one's internal state of being, and it is what we typically find to be the case in evil individuals who force themselves into being externally "good" for inner, selfish reasons. I'm not necessarily saying, however, that Job was actually this sort of evil individual; I'm merely pointing out that his external behaviors weren't necessarily indicative of an ideal state of inner development.

There is yet a third reason to believe that Job had probably not attained to a Christ-like level of psychospiritual maturity in his life. It has to do with his overly stiff and ritualistic behavior in the service of God, which is more characteristic of the immature Pharisees than it is of genuinely actualized individuals. For instance, the Bible tells us that Job routinely had his family purified after extended feasts, and that he offered a burnt sacrifice for each of his children every morning. We are further told that this was Job's "regular custom," and we can surmise from this that Job probably engaged in a whole host of other ritualistic behaviors as well. This is significant, because it tells us that Job in all likelihood had not yet adopted the ethic of creativity for himself.

It is important to understand that this ethic of creativity, which Sanford argues is the very essence of the kingdom of heaven, does not limit itself to ritualistic behaviors because it has transcended them. Rituals are intended primarily for spiritually incomplete people, who need some kind of external structure to guide their two-dimensional moral behavior in the proper direction. The ethic of developmental creativity, on the other hand, transcends this kind of subservience to ritualism because it interacts directly with the more numinous aspects of human life; it thus doesn't need a ritual to guide it in this direction because in a very important sense it has already arrived.

It is for this reason that we can take Job's ritualism to be indicative of a pre-creative ethic that was probably characterized by an inordinate degree of behavioral rigidity. This view is supported by the fact that almost all of the "good" people of Job's day were also "good" in this two-dimensional, ritualistic capacity.

Take the Pharisees of Jesus' time, for instance. They were also good in this same rigid and ritualistic way, yet they ended up condemning themselves anyway because they ignored the deeper and more relevant aspects of the inner spiritual life. But as we have seen, it is our inner state of development that ultimately matters as far as God is concerned, because it appears to be the sole criterion that will be used to determine whether or not we are worthy enough to enter the kingdom of heaven. This being the case, we simply cannot ignore our inner spiritual condition and hope to make up for it by being "good" on the outside. For if our goodness doesn't spring from within, it will ultimately be worthless, as the following indictment of the Pharisees by Jesus well illustrates:

> Woe to you, scribes and Pharisees, hypocrites! For you cleanse the outside of the cup and dish, but inside they are full of extortion and self-indulgence. Blind Pharisee, first cleanse the inside of the cup and dish, that the outside of them may be clean also. Woe to you, scribes and Pharisees, hypocrites! For you are like whitewashed tombs which indeed appear beautiful outwardly, but inside are full of dead men's bones and all uncleanness. Even so, you outwardly appear righteous to men, but inside you are full of hypocrisy and lawlessness (Matt. 23:25–28 NKJV).

From this hard-hitting passage it is clear that Jesus wants us to cleanse our innermost souls of all their accumulated "filthiness." He does *not* want us to be good in an outer sense only, because this leaves our inner depravity intact, and this is undesirable because it leaves us vulnerable to all sorts of evil influences in the future.

The question thus boils down to whether or not the external, ritualistic behavior of the Pharisees is sufficient in and of itself to lead us into the kingdom of heaven. The answer to this question, as Jesus clearly points out, is an unequivocal No! God doesn't want people who are good only on the outside; He wants people who are good on the inside also, and the reason for this isn't far to seek: all human behavior emanates from within our innermost souls, so over time we can only be as good on the outside as we are on the inside. Accordingly, unless we are clean and well-developed on the inside, our external behavior will inevitably suffer. This is why the kingdom of heaven seems to be limited to those people who have individuated to this lofty point: because they are the only individuals who can repeatedly be trusted to produce good consequences with their behavior. It is also why Jesus tells us that unless our righteousness exceeds that of the scribes and Pharisees, we will by no means enter the kingdom of heaven (Matt. 5:20). This was an especially radical message back in Jesus' day, because the scribes and Pharisees were the most honored and respected religious people in their society. A similar message today, in order to have the same effect, would have to be directed at the Pope and his hierarchy of bishops!

Jesus gives us an additional clue about the nature of our developmental goal in one of the most misunderstood verses in the entire Bible. In Matthew 5:48 He tells us to "be perfect, even as your Father in heaven is perfect." This command has caused many readers to experience a great deal of anxiety and even despair, because it is clear that we can never be perfect in this rigid, one-sided manner. St. Paul confirms this intuition by telling us that "all have sinned and fall short of the glory of God" (Rom. 3:23).

Now, Jesus was undoubtedly aware of this extreme moral shortcoming in human beings, so He almost certainly didn't believe that we could be "perfect" in this fashion. Without any further information, it seems clear that He must have had something else in mind when He originally uttered this command. And indeed, this is precisely what we find to be the case when we perform a literal translation of this passage from the original Greek. When we do this, we find that the word which is translated as "perfect" in Matt. 5:48, *teleios,* literally means "brought to its appropriate end state; wanting nothing necessary to completeness," or "fully grown and mature."

In other words, Jesus is telling us that we need to grow as much as we possibly can in our psychospiritual lives, so we can eventually become fully developed and thereby be brought to an appropriate end state. In this sense, "perfect" simply means "optimally developed." No wonder Jesus wants us to be "perfect" in this manner: because it is only by being fully developed that we can reach wholeness and thereby be fit for the kingdom of God.

Part of the task of wholeness, as we have seen, involves a unification of the disparate elements of the mind, such as the conscious ego and the unconscious Shadow. However, it also entails a unification of the other unbalanced and disconnected elements of the personality as well, and this includes the male and female sides of our innermost selves.

According to C.G. Jung, we all have both masculine and feminine aspects to our personality. The feminine side of a man is called the *anima* and the masculine side of a woman is called the *animus.* Normally, these cross-gender aspects of the mind remain suppressed and unintegrated into the larger personality, because both men and women tend to consciously identify primarily with those traits that are directly consistent with their physical gender. However, this type of inner division is not healthy, nor is it compatible with our ultimate goal of psychospiritual wholeness, because the fully developed personality is essentially *androgenous* by its very nature, which is to say that it makes more or less equal use of both masculine and feminine characteristics. Therefore, our inner quest to become whole requires that we integrate both our masculine and feminine qualities into a single androgenous unit if it is to be successful.

This is a point that is made very effectively in the Gospel of Thomas:

When you make the two into one, and when you make the inner like the outer and the outer like the inner, and the upper like the lower, and when you make male and female into a single one, so that the male will not be male nor the female be female . . . then you will enter [the kingdom] (v. 22).

Interestingly enough, we are told in this passage that our entrance into the kingdom of heaven is directly contingent upon our becoming unified on the inside. This makes good sense, because to be unified means to be fully developed and mature, and it is quite evident that heaven could never truly be heavenly if immature and irresponsible people were regularly allowed into it.[1]

Notably, however, the Bible tells us nothing about the inner status of Job's soul. It merely says that Job was good in an external, behavioral way; but even so, we are soon told that Job fell victim to a horrible series of personal calamities, which were motivated primarily by Satan and not God:

> One day the angels came to present themselves before the Lord, and Satan also came with them. The Lord said to Satan, "Where have you come from?"
>
> Satan answered the Lord, "From roaming through the earth and going back and forth in it."
>
> Then the Lord said to Satan, "Have you considered my servant Job? There is no one on earth like him; he is blameless and upright, a man who fears God and shuns evil."
>
> "Does Job fear God for nothing?" Satan replied. "Have you not put a hedge around him and his household and everything he has? You have blessed the work of his hands, so that his flocks and herds are spread throughout the land. But stretch out your hand and strike everything he has, and he will surely curse you to your face."
>
> Then the Lord said to Satan, "Very well, then, everything he has is in your hands, but on the man himself do not lay a finger."
>
> Then Satan went out from the presence of the Lord (Job 1:6–11).

It would be a mistake to understand the figure of Satan in the above passage as an external, malevolent being only. For while Satan may indeed exist somewhere in the cosmos as a concrete being, the figure of Satan mentioned above seems to be more consistent with the Law of Natural Causation, which invariably links all natural causes to their own corresponding effects.

Satan himself even gives us a hint that this is his true function in the overall universal economy. When the Lord asks him where he has come from, Satan says, "From roaming through the earth and going back and forth in it" (Job 1:7). This is an apt description of the Law of Natural Causation, which can also be said to roam through all the earth and to go back and forth in it, faithfully linking all causes with their corresponding natural effects. The "Satanic" side of this Natural Causal Law can thus be found to apply to all those efficient causes that have genuinely destructive effects in the world. In this sense it is similar to Murphy's Law, insofar as it causes everything that *can* go wrong in the world *to* go wrong eventually.

Nowhere does this Satanic side of Murphy's Law ring more true than in human life itself. For whenever things in a person's life *can* go wrong, you can bet that they *will* go wrong eventually, and that he or she will suffer "Satanic" evil as a result of it. In this case it is clear that no external being actually causes this evil to happen; the individual herself brings it about by being inwardly vulnerable to some degree of malfunctioning.

The ancient Stoic philosophers recognized that most of the events that take place in our world can ultimately be traced to this Natural Causal Law, but they had the presence of mind to associate it with God and not Satan. They realized that if God existed at all, He *had* to function as the Logos, or Logical Mediator, between cause and effect, and they further believed that this is the primary mechanism through which God is able to act in the world. For the Stoics, then, human beings were the ones who elicited efficient causes with their behavior, but it was God who faithfully linked up these humanly-inspired causes with their corresponding natural effects.

The Old Testament strongly corroborates this point of view. In the book of Isaiah, for instance, God is quoted as saying:

> I am the Lord, and there is no other. I form the light and create darkness,
> I bring prosperity and create disaster; I the Lord, do all these things
> (Isaiah 45:6–7).

Now, the only way that a good God can coherently be thought to be responsible for humanly-inspired moral evils is if He is only *indirectly* involved, perhaps at an unseen metaphysical level. In this sense God *can* be seen as being ultimately responsible for generating "Satanic" worldly events.

Interestingly enough, in Zechariah 4:10 we are given a description of the Lord that is virtually identical to the self-description of Satan that is given in Job 1:7. In this intriguing passage, we are told that the eyes of the Lord "scan to and fro throughout the whole earth" (Zech. 4:10 NKJV). But Satan also claims to be "going to and fro on the earth," and to be "walking back and forth on it" (Job 1:7, NKJV).

Now, could it be a coincidence that both God and Satan scan to and fro over the whole earth as part of their natural behavior? One would never suppose *a priori* that two such radically different beings would nevertheless be engaging in the same sort of metaphysical behavior. However, everything changes if we understand this description of Satan to be representative of the destructive "Left Hand of God." In this case, both God and Satan perform the same sort of metaphysical task because in the end they merely represent different sides of the same overall Being.

This is an interpretation of Satan that C.G. Jung would have wholeheartedly accepted, because he believed that in order to be whole, God needed Satan to function as His metaphysical opposite. Like many mystics before him, Jung believed that the four-pronged quaternity is the natural symbol of wholeness in the universe, so he became convinced that the Godhead had to therefore be comprised of four major elements. Christian theologians, however, rejected this four-pronged deity by positing a triune God (Father, Son, and Holy Spirit), whose intentions were opposed at every turn by an evil devil. In a radical move, Jung simply disagreed with this conceptualization, and posited instead that Satan was the missing fourth element of the Divine quaternity.[2]

Conventional theologians failed to consider this apparent truth, according to Jung, because their view of the Godhead was merely a projection of their own incomplete psychological makeup. According to this conceptualization, the elements of the conscious mind are unknowingly projected onto God in the form of an incomplete trinity. The Shadow is, of course, conspicuously absent from this psychological projection, because it isn't normally a part of the conscious personality. As a result, the image of God that is supposedly created by the neurotic mind is an incomplete trinity. On this Jungian view, Satan is the missing element of the Divine quaternity, just as the Shadow is the missing element of the human psyche. This is why Jung believed that God is partly evil: because he was convinced that the Godhead requires a certain amount of Satanic evil in order to be whole, just as the human personality requires the "evil" Shadow in order to be unified.

As I will be pointing out in more detail in Chapter 5, I do not believe that God has to be partly evil in order to be whole. I do, however, believe that the Biblical figure of Satan can be understood to represent the destructive "Left Hand" of God, but this doesn't necessarily require us to conclude that this Divine destructiveness is a permanent, and therefore inevitable, feature of God's true nature. This would be unspeakably catastrophic for all mortal beings, because none of us would ever stand a chance in a universe that is superintended by a partly evil deity. Rather, God's destructive side seems to be directly related to *our own* susceptibility to evil, insofar as the entire universe appears to be evil as long as we ourselves are. *Accordingly, once evil is expunged from our innermost soul, so too will God's destructive Left Hand also disappear as well.* This view presupposes that God's destructive side is metaphysically necessary because our own evil side is *itself* necessary, at least temporarily. The basic idea here is that God's destructive Left Hand is merely a reflection of *our own* temporary propensity towards evil, which won't disappear until we become fully developed on the inside.

This brings to mind an extremely important distinction concerning the various forms of evil that can possibly be said to reside in the Divine Substance. There are basically two types. On the one hand, God can be seen as being partly evil in an absolute, non-instrumental sense, so that His intrinsic wickedness would therefore remain essentially unchanged for the whole of eternity.[3] Jung would have warmly embraced this particular view, because it seems to restore the missing element of wholeness to the Divine Being.

On the other hand, God can also be seen as being "evil" in a temporary, instrumental sense only, insofar as He could be using a destructive means in order to eventually bring about a greater good. Jung would have disagreed with this more traditional interpretation of the Divine nature for three related reasons. First, this temporary, instrumental view makes evil a self-limited, non-absolute phenomenon, and this is unacceptable as long as evil is thought to be a permanently necessary ingredient in the Divine nature. The second reason why Jung would have disagreed with this instrumental view is that it effectively eliminates the metaphysical identity of evil altogether in the long run. The reason for this conclusion isn't far to seek: evil that is merely being used as a necessary means for a greater good doesn't really qualify as genuine evil in the end, since its "evil" nature presumably disappears altogether once its positive function has been fulfilled.

David Ray Griffin, of the Claremont Graduate School and School of Theology, originally introduced this useful distinction between genuine and apparent evil in his book *God, Power, and Evil*. According to Griffin, genuine evil is something that the world would have been better off without, all things considered.[4] But the world clearly would never have been better off without those necessary evils that are able to bring about greater goods. Therefore, these instrumental evils do not qualify as being genuinely evil at all. This is why the capacity to invoke instrumental evil cannot be a permanent feature of the Godhead: because instrumental evils mysteriously transform themselves into good with the passage of time.

The final reason why Jung disagreed with this instrumental interpretation of evil has to do with the horrific nature of evil itself. Jung believed that most evils are so bad that they cannot possibly be part of an underlying system of good. This is why he opposed the *privatio boni* doctrine of evil—which sees evil only as a privation of good—so vehemently: because he thought that it unduly minimized the appalling nature of evil events.

Such a conclusion, however, fails to hold up under scrutiny, because there are many types of goods that can become devilishly evil when their internal degree of wholeness or integrity is found to be lacking. Take the doomed space shuttle Challenger for instance. Its internal degree of goodness was found to be partially lacking in the form of a defective O-Ring, and it exploded during its ascent in 1986 as a result. Now, this unfortunate tragedy was clearly caused by a specific privation in the integrity of the defective O-Ring, but this fact doesn't minimize its evil impact at all. The same thing can be said of cancer, which is known to result from a privation of the good of full bodily health.

In a similar fashion, virtually all of the moral evils that have been committed by human beings throughout history can be understood to have resulted from a privation of the good of full character assembly. For just as cars, boats, and airplanes are all prone to malfunctioning when they are deprived of the good of their own full assembly, so too are human beings prone to malfunctioning (i.e., evil) when *their* characters are less than fully developed.

It is therefore quite possible for evil to retain its repugnant nature, even while maintaining its metaphysical identity as the privation of specific goods. But if this is true, then it is also possible that the apparent evils of our world are actually part of a deeper and more pervasive underlying system of good, in which case they would function as instrumental tools in the eventual production of greater goods. But this, in turn, means that it is possible that a wholly good God could actually be utilizing the apparent evils of our world to bring about greater goods. This scenario becomes all the more likely if these apparent evils are deemed to be the only logically possible means for bringing about these greater goods for humanity.

But what system of greater goods could possibly be this transcendently important to the human race? Given the strong element of necessity that seems to be tied into God's pursuit of these greater goods, it would seem that they must somehow be related to the intrinsic demands of the Human Essence. For if it is actually the case that one of the defining properties of the Human Essence is a temporary susceptibility to moral evil, then it logically follows that God cannot bring about the greater good of human existence without simultaneously putting up with the temporary production of moral evil. But if this is so, and if the greater good of human existence is deemed to be sufficiently valuable, then God would clearly be morally justified in creating humanity, despite the temporary existence of moral evil.

But why should the temporary existence of evil be necessarily entailed by the specific properties of the Human Essence? The answer to this question, as we have seen before, gets back to the need for a self-directed developmental process in human beings. To the extent that this is so, then there must logically come a point near the beginning of this developmental process where human beings are both morally and epistemologically immature. *It is this moral and epistemological immaturity that results in the temporary production of moral evil, because these dual characteristics necessarily make us too ignorant and too immature to be able to reliably avoid producing destructive consequences with our behavior.*

Fortunately, the developmental process itself also ensures that one day in the distant future moral evil will cease to be a problem for humanity, for once individual humans reach a state of optimal character growth for themselves, they will automatically have more than enough knowledge and moral fiber to be able to consistently avoid producing evil with their behavior. There are two reasons for this. First, one cannot be reliably counted upon to avoid producing evil consequences with one's behavior until one first knows *how* to do so, but this cannot happen until one has amassed a huge quantity of practical knowledge pertaining to the actual avoidance of evil. This knowledge can only come about in response to a self-actualizing process of personal individuation. Secondly, one cannot be reliably counted upon to avoid evil until one has become morally developed enough to *want* to be able to do so deep inside of one's heart. But this too can only happen as a consequence of full character development.

We see, then, that it is our own state of psychospiritual development that turns out to be the single greatest factor in determining how much moral evil exists in the world. This is why God has apparently subordinated everything in our world to the eventual attainment of our individuation, including the temporary existence of pain and suffering. This leads us to consider one of the greatest ironies of human existence; namely, that the only way we can be cured of our propensity for evil is by first experiencing it directly (in the sense of initially existing in an immature state), because we can't overcome our inner evil until we first exist in the immediate presence of it.

That is to say, we have to first exist in the midst of evil (due once again to the intrinsic demands of the Human Essence) before we can grow mature enough to be able to minimize our own contribution to the suffering of the world. This is a kind of "spiritual homeopathy" where "like cures like," where we first have to suffer evil consequences before we can eventually become developed enough to cease causing them. This would explain why a wholly good God could nevertheless utilize *prima facie* evils to produce greater goods: because this appears to be the only logically possible way for mature humans to be created *ex nihilo*.

Our world view thus depends in large part on how we conceptualize the evil that takes place every day in our world. If we view it as an absolute metaphysical phenomenon that finds its ultimate home in God's underlying nature, our world view is bound to be pessimistic and even downright ominous, since God would then be rendered partly evil for the rest of eternity. On the other hand, if we view evil as a necessary means to a greater good, our world view suddenly becomes *much* more optimistic and hopeful, because it means that we are all suffering for a transcendently good, and therefore justifiable, reason.

Everything thus turns on whether or not we believe that part of God is absolutely evil, or whether we believe that God's destructive side is merely an essential tool for the attainment of a greater good. Indeed, the existence of God's omnibenevolence, which is one of His most important attributes, rests squarely on how we choose to answer this question. A God that is partly evil in a non-instrumental, absolute sense clearly cannot be all-good, no matter how this evil is interpreted. On the other hand, a God that merely uses an evil means to bring about a greater good can coherently be thought of as an omnibenevolent Being, especially if there is no other logically possible way to bring about this greater good. Again, this is because necessary evils that are used to promote greater goods are themselves transformed into good in the end.

This is an immensely encouraging piece of news, for if the human developmental process is postulated to be the greater good that God is aiming for, and if worldly evil is postulated to be the result of those essential human properties that *must* be instantiated if genuine humans are to be capable of existing, then *all* of the world's evil will eventually be transformed into good in the end, either directly or indirectly.

Of course, I don't mean to say that each individual evil event that takes place in our world is necessary in and of itself for the eventual attainment of this greater good. This is clearly an absurd position, because it is hard to see how the rape of a defenseless baby, for instance, can possibly be necessary in and of itself for the realization of any type of greater good. Everything changes, however, if we shift our focus away from individual events themselves and towards the underlying structural features of our world that make evil events possible in the first place, because these structural features can themselves be necessary for the greater good without each individual event that takes place because of them being necessary in any larger sense. *We must therefore distinguish between the structural features of our world that are necessary for human existence, and the individual events that take place because of them, which are merely contingent.*

Free will, for instance, is generally considered to be one of the most important structural features of our present world order, but this doesn't at all mean that the evil events that take place because of free will are equally necessary in and of themselves. They are only necessary in a very indirect way, when they are viewed *in terms of* the underlying freedom that makes them possible, because it is human freedom that is necessary for the attainment of the greatest overall good, and not any specific event that takes undue advantage of this particular metaphysical characteristic.

I believe that a coherent theodicy can indeed be built around this instrumental view of evil, insofar as the various destructive events that take place in our world can be viewed in terms of an underlying series of structural parameters, which are *themselves* indispensable to the attainment of the greatest possible good for humanity. To the extent that this conceptualization is accurate, the so-called dark side of God cannot be genuinely evil, since it is necessarily being employed in the service of bringing about the greatest possible good for the human race, which can be said to be the goal of full character development for all individuals. Indeed, insofar as this transcendent form of goodness cannot be obtained without a certain amount of "evil" emanating from the Godhead (due once again to the intrinsic demands of the Human Definition), we find that this *prima facie* evil isn't really evil at all, because it is actually a logically necessary ingredient in the production of the greatest possible good for humanity.

There is a statement in the Gospel of Thomas that supports this essentialistic interpretation of the temporary necessity of evil:

> Jesus said, "The father's kingdom is like a person who has [good] seed. His enemy came at night and sowed weeds among the good seed. The person did not let them pull up the weeds, but said to them, 'No, or you might go to pull up the weeds and pull up the wheat along with them.' For on the day of the harvest the weeds will be conspicuous and will be pulled up and burned" (v. 57).

This insightful passage supports the idea that there is a necessary tie-in between good and evil in our world; so much so, in fact, that evil *cannot* be eliminated at this point in time without a simultaneous elimination of the good taking place as well. This is why the weeds in the above example couldn't be uprooted without a simultaneous loss of the wheat transpiring: because good and evil, symbolized by the wheat and weeds respectively, are for some reason necessarily tied to one another at this early stage in our development. To the extent that this is so, it means that evil is in some sense metaphysically necessary for the eventual attainment of the good. For the Developmental Theist, this translates into the idea that evil is necessarily (though temporarily) entailed by the various essential properties of the Human Definition.

It is inconceivable that a perfectly good and all-powerful God could knowingly create darkness and bring about unnecessary (i.e., genuine) evil in the world. On the other hand, such a benevolent Creator could possibly choose to bring about a certain amount of necessary evil in human affairs without being morally indictable for it, but *only* if this evil is genuinely required in an instrumental sense in order to bring about the greatest possible good for humanity.

One of the great boons of this instrumental perspective is that it enables us to preserve the absolute monotheism of God in the face of worldly evil, because God Himself is seen as being the ultimate cause of all forms of destructiveness. The ancient Hebrews strongly affirmed this uncompromising monotheism, which was something that Hebrew scholars around the time of Jesus refused to do, largely because they felt uncomfortable attributing all worldly evil ultimately to God. As a consequence, they utilized the figure of Satan to take most of the blame for the world's evil. This is theologically unacceptable, however, because if Satan really existed as an external evil power in the world, and if he truly had the capacity to oppose God by unilaterally bringing about genuine evil in human society, then we would have a profound dualism on our hands, in which the goodness of God would be pitted against the evil power of Satan. This kind of full-scale dualism is totally unacceptable to the committed monotheist, and for good reason: either God is directly sovereign over the entire universe, including the devil, or else He is not. If the first situation is correct, then it becomes difficult (but not impossible) to explain why a good God would allow so much evil to exist in the world. If, on the other hand, the second situation is correct, we then have an irrational dualistic phenomenon to contend with that totally invalidates the omnipotence of God, and thereby directly contradicts the strong monotheistic traditions of our forefathers, including those of Judaism, Christianity, and Islam. (Please refer to Chapter 4 for more concerning the many conceptual advantages of monotheism over dualism.)

Fortunately, there is a third alternative that enables us to coherently maintain our belief in a perfectly good monotheistic Creator, despite all the evil that exists in the world. This is the alternative that places the ultimate responsibility for evil, not on Satan, but on the eternally existing Human Definition, which God freely chose to instantiate in our world. On this view, God chose to instantiate the Human Essence because of the infinite amount of good that it will eventually end up achieving in the universe. Unfortunately, the Human Essence also contains the temporary propensity for evil as well, as we have seen, but since no other essence was apparently good enough to fulfill God's lofty expectations, God opted to instantiate the Human Essence *despite* its temporary proclivity for evil.[5]

What this means is that God as omnipotent[6] freely chose to create a situation in which evil must temporarily exist in the world, not because He wanted to bring about evil for its own sake, but because He *had* to temporarily create evil in order to bring about all the good that He wants to eventually exist.[7] Satan can thus be understood, at least in part, as the spiritual personification of God's destructive "Left Hand," which *must* be temporarily evil if it is to be capable of producing the greatest amount of good in human life.

To the extent that this hypothesis is valid, however, it isn't quite accurate to term this Divine destructiveness as genuine evil, because the overall state of affairs in which it occurs is presumably the only logically possible way there is to achieve the greatest amount of good in the world, at least with respect to the instantiation of the Human Essence. *It is thus the spectre of an absolute Cosmic Necessity that protects our perfectly good God from the accusation that He is also partly evil.* For if it is the case that only one possible state of affairs is intrinsically good enough to fulfill the Divine Will, and if it is also the case that this one state of affairs also inevitably contains a temporary (and self-limited) amount of evil, then it follows that a perfectly good God could in fact bring about this mixture of good and evil without being morally indictable for it, since He would ultimately be aiming for the greatest possible amount of good in human affairs.

Once again, this instrumental perspective seems to preserve God's goodness at the expense of His all-power, but this is arguably an appearance only. For if it is truly the case that the temporary existence of evil is necessarily entailed by humanity's various essential properties, and if no other human-like essence is deemed to have been worth creating in the eyes of God, then God's omnipotence *cannot* be impugned by the temporary existence of moral evil in the world, because the Human Essence cannot properly exist without the simultaneous existence of evil (since evil, on this essentialistic view, is temporarily entailed by humanity's own essential properties). But if this is so, then it becomes logically impossible for God to have instantiated the Human Essence without a simultaneous instantiation of moral evil. And since the prospect of Divine omnipotence isn't generally thought to be limited by inherently contradictory acts, then God's all-power cannot be said to be compromised by the temporary existence of evil in the world, at least not as long as some form of moral evil is held to be a necessary consequence of humanity's essential properties.

What this means is that the intrinsic properties of the Human Essence require God to temporarily exhibit a dreaded "dark side," because the instantiation of humanity automatically brings with it a world of self-limited evil at the same time. Within this evil context, Satan can be seen to exist in the form of an obstacle or stumbling block on the way to personal wholeness. This is consistent, as we have seen, with a literal interpretation of the word "satan," which means "adversary" or "stumbling block." The adversarial stumbling block in this instance is simply the evil side of creation that must temporarily exist if the greatest amount of good is to be able to come into being.

Within this developmental, teleological perspective, the word of the Lord in Job 1:8 can be understood to represent the superficial appearance of things, which sees goodness and badness only as a function of how something appears on the outside. This explains why God sees Job as such a perfect and upright man, when in fact Job was probably far from this lofty goal on the inside, as we all inevitably are, since everyone sins and falls short of the glory of God (Rom. 3:23).

It is the figure of Satan, however, who looks deeper than mere appearances. This is why he symbolizes the destructive side of God's overall nature: because he looks on the innermost heart of human beings, which predisposes them to all sorts of evil influences. This predisposition towards evil occurs because the human character structure is only partially developed at the present time, and anything that is partially developed tends to malfunction with the passage of time. This explains why the "Satanic" side of God argues that Job is only good because of his fortunate external circumstances: because partially developed human beings tend to be "good" primarily for superficial reasons only.

In other words, God, acting via the Law of Natural Causation, looks on the innermost heart of man and brings into being that which is naturally called for. It is thus the "Satanic" side of God that surveys all the possibilities on the earth and metes out evil whenever it is appropriate. This is why the Bible tells us that God, disguised as Satan, goes about as a "roaring lion, seeking whom he may devour." Lions characteristically move about looking for the appropriate prey to pounce on, and so does this Satanic image of natural causality: it constantly roams about the earth searching for spiritually vulnerable people to "devour."

Satan thus serves an indispensable role in God's Universal Economy, because in the end, he appears to be a spiritual personification of God's destructive, but nonetheless essential, Left Hand. This is why Satan is allowed into the immediate presence of God amongst the other angels: because as an essential part of God's overall nature, he has an important job to accomplish. If Satan were the intrinsically evil being that many people like to think he is, God would never have allowed him into the court of heaven to begin with, nor would He have allowed Satan to originally tempt humanity in the Garden of Eden. But Satan clearly *was* allowed to tempt Adam and Eve, and he clearly *was* allowed into God's heavenly court, because in actuality he is an essential part of God's Creative Plan.

We can therefore say that Satan is the archetype of real-world causality, who ceaselessly tests the developmental integrity of all individuals, and who subsequently rewards everyone with their just due in life. In this sense, Satan can be thought of as the spiritual executor of Murphy's Law, who sees to it that everything that *can* go wrong in life *will* go wrong eventually. He does this because he rewards all of our spiritual impurities and developmental inadequacies with their corresponding logical effects in the world.

The answer to this kind of ontological satan is clearly a rigorous program of self-development, in which one does everything in one's power to grow to the point that one can naturally prevent this kind of self-inflicted evil from occurring. This is the "whole armor of God" that St. Paul speaks of in his letter to the Ephesians, whose basic function is to prevent the "satan" of natural causality from having an "in" to one's personality, through the development of a sufficient amount of inner strength and moral fortitude:

> Finally, my brethren, be strong in the Lord, and in the power of his might. Put on the whole armour of God, that ye may be able to stand against the wiles of the devil. For we wrestle not against flesh and blood, but against principalities, against powers, against the rulers of the darkness of this world, against spiritual wickedness in high *places*. Wherefore take unto you the whole armour of God, that ye may be able to withstand in the evil day, and having done all, to stand. Stand therefore, having your loins girt about with truth, and having on the breastplate of righteousness; And your feet shod with the preparation of the gospel of peace; Above all, taking

the shield of faith, wherewith ye shall be able to quench all the fiery darts of the wicked. And take the helmet of salvation, and the sword of the Spirit, which is the word of God: Praying always with all prayer and supplication in the Spirit, and watching thereunto with all perseverance and supplication for all saints (Eph. 6:10–18, KJV).

Although St. Paul in the above passage seems to be attributing the cause of evil to an external devil, these wicked "principalities" in "high places" can also be seen to be perfectly consistent with an internal devil. Certainly there is no pressing reason to believe that the "rulers of the darkness of this world" have to be external beings from another realm. They can also plausibly be identified with the many different psychopathologies that are known to afflict the human mind, especially since we know that it is *human beings* who are actually ruling our world through their own psychospiritual faculties. And indeed, an in-depth psychological examination of such evil rulers as Hitler and Mussolini readily reveals a wealth of wicked and destructive tendencies that are almost entirely explicable within the present body of psychiatric knowledge.

Take Adolph Hitler for instance. He is known to have suffered from the bizarre psychiatric malady known as *necrophilia*, or the love of the dead. Armed with this highly perverted character disorder, Hitler was able to respond to many of his internal prejudices with an unprecedented degree of cruelty and destruction, *and we don't really need to resort to extraterrestrial explanations in order to account for this profound level of wickedness.* An especially good study of this relationship between human psychopathology and moral evil can be found in Erich Fromm's *The Anatomy of Human Destructiveness*.[8]

It is for this reason that the whole armor of God is such an effective antidote against the inner wiles of the devil: because it is really a synonym for the many psychospiritual defenses against evil that can readily be mustered by the self-actualizing individual, who as a consequence has an extremely wide range of evil-defusing tools at her disposal. In other words, the whole armor of God is the development of a moral and responsible character structure, which is naturally possessed with a substantial amount of inner strength and moral fortitude. The reason for this, of course, is that relatively few things can go wrong in a person who is well-developed on the inside. This is why the Bible tells us that Satan will flee from those who resist him: because in the very act of resisting him, one tends to automatically grow stronger and more mature in one's life, and it is this greater level of self-development that automatically tends to make one less vulnerable overall to the destructive hand of natural causality.

Although it is impossible to say for sure whether or not this naturalistic interpretation of Satan is in fact the correct one (at least as far as the story of Job is concerned), one thing is obvious: each and every one of the calamities that befalls Job can be fully explained in a naturalistic fashion, which is to say that they can all be explained in terms of the normal, everyday forces of causation that are known to constantly be at work throughout our world. This means that it isn't strictly necessary to resort to a supernatural explanation for this type of "satanic" evil, because a naturalistic one will actually do the job quite nicely. Indeed, Occam's Principle of Theoretical Economy *compels* us to accept this naturalistic interpretation of the role of Satan, because it is inherently much simpler than its supernatural counterpart.

With this in mind, we will now take a deeper look at the various tragedies that rapidly befall our friend Job:

> One day when Job's sons and daughters were feasting and drinking wine at the oldest brother's house, a messenger came to Job and said, "The oxen were plowing and the donkeys were grazing nearby, and the Sabeans attacked and carried them off. They put the servants to the sword, and I am the only one who has escaped to tell you!"
>
> While he was still speaking, another messenger came and said, "The fire of God fell from the sky and burned up the sheep and the servants, and I am the only one who has escaped to tell you!"
>
> While he was still speaking, another messenger came and said, "The Chaldeans formed three raiding parties and swept down on your camels and carried them off. They put the servants to the sword, and I am the only one who has escaped to tell you!"
>
> While he was still speaking, yet another messenger came and said, "Your sons and daughters were feasting and drinking wine at the oldest brother's house, when suddenly a mighty wind swept in from the desert and struck the four corners of the house. It collapsed on them and they are dead, and I am the only one who has escaped to tell you!"
>
> At this, Job got up and tore his robe and shaved his head. Then he fell to the ground in worship and said: "Naked I came from my mother's womb, and naked I will depart. The Lord gave and the Lord has taken away; may the name of the Lord be praised."
>
> In all this, Job did not sin by charging God with wrongdoing (Job 1:13–22).

It is interesting to note, once again, that each of the calamities mentioned above has a clearly defined natural cause associated with it, except possibly for the "fire of God" that fell from the sky and burned up Job's sheep and servants. On the other hand, this fire of God could easily have had a naturalistic explanation for it as well. Several different types of natural phenomena could possibly fit this description, including meteor showers, lightning strikes, and even fiery, volcano-induced atmospheric disturbances. This latter possibility is particularly noteworthy, as a number of different volcanic eruptions throughout history have been known to rain fire down from the sky, even hundreds of miles away from the eruption. Volcanic eruptions on the Greek island of Santorini, for instance, have been directly witnessed by a number of credible observers over the years, many of whom claimed to have seen fiery discharges rain from the sky for days following an eruption. Indeed, it is widely believed that the Biblical plagues of ancient Egypt may have been caused by a particularly violent eruption of Santorini's volcano.

The important take-home point here is that one doesn't *have* to attribute the underlying causation of worldly evil to Satan alone; one can simply attribute it to the natural cause-and-effect order of the physical universe, which clearly has a great deal of destructiveness built into it. To the extent that this interpretation of satanic evil is accurate, the use of Satan as an explanatory device in the Bible may simply reflect the destructive side of natural causation, as we have seen.

The process of socialization forms an integral part of this "satanic" power for extreme destruction. We can say this because of the immense power of the society-building process, which is able to duplicate most of the moral evils that have been previously attributed to Satan and his cohorts. As a consequence, we no longer need a supernatural being to account for the many self-inflicted evils that take place daily on our planet, because the natural forces that are inherent in human society are more than sufficient to do the trick. These forces have the power to concentrate, and thereby to magnify, the evil tendencies of any given population, because they work in concert with the human mind's own evil-creating capacities. The process itself works like this: evil (i.e., pathological and destructive) socialization policies naturally give rise to evil minds, which subsequently act to make the original socialization policies worse for the next generation of youngsters, who then turn out to be more wicked than the preceding generation, and so on. This evil-magnifying process continues to build on itself in a vicious cycle that slowly escalates from generation to generation, until it eventually reaches a fever pitch and endangers the existence of the entire society itself. This is one of the ways in which the sins of the father are passed on to subsequent generations.[9]

This is why it is so important to take our culture's socialization policies seriously, because even the smallest negative influences can become greatly magnified over time by other synergistic forces in society. As a direct consequence of these interacting forces, we can say that the sum total of a society's capacity for evoking evil responses from its citizens is largely the consequence of the many destructive socialization policies that are at work within it. This observation becomes all the more significant and ominous when we realize that even the simplest of human societies makes use of hundreds of socialization techniques to mold their citizenry, so we're talking about a *huge* capacity to bring about evil in the world, not as a function of a demonic intervention into worldly events *per se*, but purely as a function of humanity's own naturalistic capacity to bring evil into existence.

This appears to be precisely what happened in Nazi Germany. A wide variety of social, political, and psychological factors came together to produce one of the most evil and destructive regimes in the entire history of our planet. But if it is true that the overwhelming evil of the Nazis can be sufficiently explained in a naturalistic fashion, without recourse to a supernatural devil, then there would appear to be no compelling reason to invoke the activity of such a devil in *any* instance of moral evil in the world, since the evil that was typified by the Nazis seems to represent the very pinnacle of humanity's evil-making capacity.

We mustn't forget that we humans have a great deal in common with the Biblical figure of Satan; so much so, in fact, that he could literally *be* us on a deep spiritual level. After all, we too are immensely powerful spiritual creatures who, like Satan, originally fell from God's Grace. Indeed, we are the most powerful spiritual creatures that we know about in the *entire universe* as far as our own ability to create evil is concerned. There is little doubt, for instance, that we are having a devilishly evil effect on the rest of the biosphere, because we are single-handedly doing our best to pollute and pillage our way out of existence. To the rest of the animal kingdom, then, we must appear to be very satanic indeed. In fact, if our zoological brethren could become consciously aware of the many evil influences that we are routinely bringing about in the world, they would undoubtedly be convinced that *we* are the true devils who are at work on this planet, and *not* Satan and his cohorts.

In short, then, while it is possible that a literal being by the name of Satan is the deliberate cause of worldly evil, it doesn't seem to be very likely, given the fact that we can explain the vast majority of evil events entirely through naturalistic means. Earthquakes, for instance, are easily explained by means of naturalistic forces within the earth's crust, which act to oppose one another until one of the forces overwhelms the other and an earthquake results. The same thing can be said for hurricanes and tornadoes, which occur when the well-understood climatological forces in the earth's atmosphere make them inevitable. It would seem, then, that the only place where an external spiritual being could possibly be involved in the genesis of natural evil is in the initial design of the physical world itself, which is what makes this sort of physical destructiveness possible in the first place. But of course, it is God who is responsible for this initial design, and not Satan.

This same sort of argument can be applied to human destructiveness as well. People act in immoral ways, not because an external being is unknowingly coercing their behavior in a destructive fashion, but because of well-understood psychological and sociological processes that compel them to act in this manner. Satan as an external being seems to have no role in the genesis of these destructive behaviors, because it is the underlying design of the human mind that is clearly at fault in these instances. Again, though, it is God who is responsible for this initial design, and not Satan.

The orthodox theist, of course, is not threatened by our evil-prone situation in this world because she believes that it was created for a good, and therefore fully justifiable, reason. Indeed, she believes that this reason is so transcendently worthwhile that it will ultimately end up justifying all the evils that have ever occurred on this planet (not in terms of each contingent evil in itself, but rather in terms of the necessary structure of the world that makes these contingent evils possible). But if this is so, then the cause of these worldly evils wouldn't necessarily have to be an evil spiritual being by the name of Satan; it could just as easily be the natural cause and effect order of the world itself that is responsible for causing them. Indeed, to the extent that this is actually the case, the use of Satan as an explanatory mechanism for worldly evil could merely turn out to be a literary device whose function has simply been to personify the many types of evils that human beings are naturally prone to.

There is no doubt that this sort of personification in the Bible has served a good purpose over the years, because it has made the concept of evil accessible and tangible to millions of pre-literate people who would have otherwise not been capable of understanding it nearly as well. Most of these individuals were simply incapable of understanding the many complex causal patterns that are involved in the true genesis of evil, so the Biblical writers gave them a personified image of evil that they *were* in fact capable of understanding and relating to. Best of all, the net effect of this personification device turned out to be much the same as if they had understood the true genesis of worldly evil all along, since it effectively taught them that evil actually exists in the world, and that it should be vigorously opposed with all of one's might. Indeed, to the extent that this explanatory scenario is accurate, the use of this personification device in the Bible must be seen as being eminently justifiable in the end, because it is always better to speak to people where they are at (i.e., on their own level of understanding), instead of overwhelming them with highly complex technical matters that they can't possibly relate to. This is why the technique of speaking in parables, as Jesus did, is so timelessly effective as a transcultural teaching device: because parables contain deeper levels of truth that are seamlessly embedded in real-world examples that everyone everywhere can relate to.

Even today, the use of personification as a teaching device is justifiable in those instances where people cannot properly understand the concept of evil otherwise. It is better, all things considered, for a person to know about evil through a personal devil than it is for them to not know about evil at all. On the other hand, there are millions of intellectually sophisticated people in the world today who are quite capable of distinguishing between natural and supernatural causes of evil. As far as these individuals are concerned, the use of Satan as a personification device is *not* so expedient, because it tends to lead them away from theism. The reason for this negative effect is clear, for when these reality-oriented individuals see that worldly evils occur because of entirely naturalistic processes, and not because of an external devil *per se*, they will tend to disbelieve any religion that would have originally given rise to such a pre-modern concept of evil.

There is yet one more facet to this personification device that is strongly counterproductive, even if one sincerely believes that the devil exists: it tends to lead one to shift the ultimate blame—and hence the responsibility—for evil from one's own free will to a malicious devil. This being the case, it tends to lessen a person's overall motivation for change, since it seems to suggest that it is Satan, and not the individual himself, who is ultimately at fault whenever a sinful behavior occurs. On the other hand, if one feels compelled to resist the devil by changing one's behavior for the better, as the Bible suggests we do, then this personification device will have ended up serving its function well. There is a problem, however, with this particular mechanism for personal change: few people feel seriously compelled to change when another being is thought to be responsible for their bad behavior, and this becomes especially true if that being cannot be seen, heard, or felt.

To his supreme credit, Job refused to blame an external devil for his personal suffering. He chose instead to maintain his faith in God no matter what happened to him. He realized that, just as he came into this world with nothing, so too will he also depart with nothing when his earthly life is finished. These are timeless words of wisdom that we would do well to learn from today.

The Relationship Between Knowledge and Evil

We must continue to bear in mind that Satan, acting through the Principle of Natural Causation, is 100 percent thorough, and therefore unbearably ruthless, as long as we continue to engage in destructive behaviors. That is to say, he will not stop until he rewards *all* of the destructive causes that we engage in with their corresponding logical effects. In the process, he makes certain that everything that *can* go wrong in our lives *will* go wrong eventually.

This realization is immensely important, because it links a great deal of human suffering to ignorance, immaturity, and poor living habits. The reasoning behind this linkage is clear, for as long as we persist in being ignorant and immature, we will continue to live our lives in a destructive and unhealthful fashion, and this, in turn, will naturally make us susceptible to all sorts of evil influences in our lives. This is the price we have to pay for being free-willed agents in a world that is ruled by unforgiving natural laws that are fixed in time and space.[10]

The Bible makes it clear that it is ignorance that is responsible for causing most of the destructiveness in human life:

> My people are destroyed for lack of knowledge. Because you have rejected knowledge, I also reject you as my priests; because you have ignored the law of your God, I also will ignore your children (Hosea 4:6).

This is undoubtedly one of the most remarkable passages in the entire Bible, insofar as it ties our rejection of knowledge to our own personal destruction. This is significant, because the vast majority of evil effects in our world are clearly produced by our own lack of knowledge about the types of behaviors that we *should* be engaging in during our lives on this planet. In this sense knowledge can be seen to be intimately related to wisdom, because wisdom can be considered to be properly directed knowledge.

It is the faculty of clear and accurate thought that is able to manufacture wisdom from mere knowledge, since it is able to weave a higher sense of morality from the basic facts of life. No one was more aware of this intimate relationship between morality and human thought than the French mathematician and philosopher Blaise Pascal, as we can see from the following sagacious passage:

> Man is only a reed, the feeblest reed in nature, but he is a thinking reed. There is no need for the entire universe to arm itself in order to annihilate him: a vapor, a drop of water, suffices to kill him. But were the universe to crush him, man would yet be more noble than that which slays him, because he knows that he dies, and the advantage the universe has over him; of this the universe knows nothing. Thus all our dignity lies in thought. By thought we must raise ourselves, not by space and time, which we cannot fill. Let us strive, then, to think well—therein is the principle of morality.[11]

But even if we are able to think well, so we can thereby accurately determine what the good happens to be in any given instance, we still need to know *how* to best attain it, and this can prove to be very difficult indeed. This is why it is so important for us to be able to possess the right type of practical knowledge in our day-to-day lives: because our ability to maximize the good is directly dependent upon it. It would therefore be a mistake to assume that most instances of good are easily attainable, or that all we need to do to attain them is to possess the proper amount of desire. Unfortunately, this isn't always the case, because more often than not, the good is comprised of a complicated mix of behaviors that requires a good deal of practical knowledge before it can be effectively brought about.

The trials and tribulations of parenthood provide a good case in point. Most parents want to treat their children in the best possible way, but relatively few mothers and fathers know how to precisely go about doing this. For some, being "good" to their children means spanking them on a daily basis, while for others it means leaving them alone as much as possible to teach them personal responsibility. Neither instance is optimal as far as the children themselves are concerned, but the parents don't know how to act any better, so they don't. The children, however, are inevitably damaged by this sort of destructive (though well-intentioned) upbringing, and they tend to exhibit this damage through their own maladaptive behaviors when they grow up.

We are clearly placing a very large premium on the intrinsic value of knowledge and understanding, due to their combined ability to combat moral evil. Not surprisingly, the Bible also concurs on this vital point as well, as Job himself explains:

"But where can wisdom be found? Where does understanding dwell? Man does not comprehend its worth; it cannot be found in the land of the living. The deep says, 'It is not in me'; the sea says, 'It is not with me.' It cannot be bought with the finest gold, nor can its price be weighed in silver. It cannot be bought with the gold of Ophir, with precious onyx or sapphires. Neither gold nor crystal can compare with it, nor can it be had for jewels of gold. Coral and jasper are not worthy of mention; the price of wisdom is beyond rubies. The topaz of Cush cannot compare with it; it cannot be bought with pure gold. Where then does wisdom come from? Where does understanding dwell? It is hidden from the eyes of every living thing, concealed even from the birds of the air. Destruction and Death say, 'Only a rumor of it has reached our ears.' God understands the way to it and he alone knows where it dwells, for He views the ends of the earth and sees everything under the heavens. When He established the force of the wind and measured out the waters, when He made a decree for the rain and a path for the thunderstorm, then He looked at wisdom and appraised it; He confirmed it and tested it. And He said to man, 'The fear of the Lord—that is wisdom, and to shun evil is understanding'" (Job 28:12–28).

There is no question, then, that the Bible places the highest possible priority on wisdom and understanding, and in Job 28:28 we're told why: because it enables us to "shun evil." This remarkable statement leaves little doubt that as far as the Old Testament is concerned, the transcendent function of knowledge and understanding is to enable us to avoid producing moral evils with our behavior.[12]

Indeed, the Bible even goes so far as to assert that God Himself will reject those who reject knowledge, as the previously quoted passage from Hosea points out (Hosea 4:6). This might seem to indicate to some that it is God Himself who is responsible for causing the initial act of rejection, but this isn't true at all, because God chooses to "reject" us only *after* we have first chosen to reject a knowledge of the good in our lives. This rejection then leads directly to all sorts of maladaptive behavior patterns, which in turn lead to a wide range of destructive consequences. This is why God rejects those who reject knowledge: because a rejection of knowledge inevitably leads to ignorant behaviors, which then culminate in destructive (i.e., evil) effects.

In other words, it isn't as if God directly turns His back on us when we reject knowledge. It is, rather, the *cumulative result* of our ignorance that makes it seem *as though* God has turned His back on us, because by being ignorant in our day-to-day lives, we naturally bring about certain destructive situations in our lives that naturally make God seem distant from us. In reality, though, He is just as close to us as He has always been. We, on the other hand, have effectively removed ourselves *from Him* by choosing to be so ignorant of the good; and this, in turn, exonerates God from the responsibility for most of the evil in our world. Instead, the responsibility for this evil is placed squarely on *our own* shoulders. The book of Isaiah confirms this important point in the following insightful passage:

> Behold, the Lord's hand is not shortened, that it cannot save; nor His ear heavy, that it cannot hear. But your iniquities have separated you from your God; and your sins have hidden His face from you, so that He will not hear. For your hands are defiled with blood, and your fingers with iniquity; your lips have spoken lies, your tongue has muttered perversity. No one calls for justice, nor does any plead for truth. They trust in empty words and speak lies; they conceive evil and bring forth iniquity (Isa. 59:1–4 NKJV).

It is possible, however, to turn things around by putting the ultimate responsibility for evil back on God, since He is the one who originally designed and created our evil-prone world to begin with. This retort is valid even if we take a literal view of the Fall in the Garden of Eden, for while Adam and Eve may have inspired the Fall with their own transgression of God's command, it was nevertheless God's "fault" for creating them in such a vulnerable state to begin with. The same thing can be said for the serpent's contribution to the whole affair, since God knew from the very beginning that the serpent would lead them into disobedience, yet He allowed this devious creature into the Garden of Eden anyway.

The only way out of this mess, and to thereby take God "off the hook" as far as the present existence of evil is concerned, is to appeal to some type of larger cosmic necessity, which would have functioned to severely constrain the way human beings themselves could be created, *vis-à-vis* the necessary nature of the world itself. This sort of theoretical maneuver is actually part of an old philosophical tradition known as *essentialism*, which a great many respected thinkers throughout history, including Plato, Aquinas, and Plantinga, have believed in. This essentialist way of thinking is able to exonerate God of the responsibility for evil because it says that things *necessarily* have to be the way they presently are (at least temporarily) if we are to truly be free, and therefore fully human.

It is also able to preserve God's omnipotence in the face of evil as well, because all the power in the universe cannot overcome an absolute state of metaphysical necessity when such a state actually exists. To illustrate, there is no conceivable amount of power that could make two plus two equal seven, because this arithmetic relation is necessarily true in and of itself. Similarly, there is no amount of power that could remove evil from the world if evil is a necessary ingredient in its composition. This would be the case if humans necessarily had to be both free and initially ignorant (i.e., epistemologically immature) in order to be genuinely human, and if God nevertheless wanted to create a world of humans because of their intrinsic value as free, self-determining beings.

We mustn't be fooled, however, into believing that knowledge alone is all that is required to bring about the good in our lives; we also have to *want* to produce the good with all of our might. This latter ingredient is known as *morality*. There are thus two vital components to bringing about the best possible state of affairs in our lives: 1) the inner desire to produce it, which is morality, and 2) the knowledge of how to go about producing it, which is wisdom. Actually, these two components are intimately interrelated with one another, since a moral desire for the good typically leads us to desire more evil-attenuating knowledge, while an advanced knowledge of the good typically inspires us to desire our own optimal state of moral development.

The key to becoming moral enough to desire the good in all possible circumstances is being optimally developed in a psychospiritual sense. This is because the closer we grow towards our goal of individuation, the more moral we will automatically become by definition. At the same time, our psychospiritual growth also brings with it additional knowledge about *how* to best go about producing good with our behavior.

This is why psychiatrist M. Scott Peck can say that spiritual growth is the ultimate answer to the problem of evil. It is also why he can call laziness the ultimate or "original" sin. For if the good is a complex conglomeration of behaviors that requires a good deal of foresight and effort to bring about, then anything that blocks this process can properly be called evil. And what could possibly hinder these good-producing behaviors more than personal laziness?

Unfortunately, the natural tendency of all physical systems, including human beings, is to always revert back to the lowest possible energy state. Thus, all physical systems are intrinsically lazy by their very constitution. Consequently, in order to bring about the good, we must first find a way to compensate for the intrinsic laziness of our bodies. This is the function of pain and suffering, for when we are hurt on a deep spiritual level, we are naturally motivated to overcome our pain by doing whatever we possibly can to eliminate it.

In this sense, psychospiritual growth is a process of pain-inspired *negative reinforcement,* insofar as the pain we experience in our day-to-day lives inherently drives us to do whatever we can to get rid of it. It is this elimination of pain that is the very hallmark of negative reinforcement, because it is the *removal* of our suffering that makes us feel so much better.

This conclusion, however, begs the deeper question of why God had to create such an inherently "lazy" physical system to begin with. Indeed, it is possible to imagine a very different state of affairs obtaining, had God created an entropy-reducing system that naturally would have sought out the highest energy state possible, because then our constitutions wouldn't have been so inherently lazy, and as a consequence, we wouldn't have had to struggle so hard to achieve higher levels of personal growth. There are, however, two severe problems with this suggestion. First, the underlying character of our entire physical universe would have clearly been irrevocably changed had it been entropy-reducing by its very nature, because matter would have then been supercharged with energy all the time. This of course would have vastly increased the reactivity of all physical substances in existence, which in turn would have grossly destabilized our entire world, even to the point of rendering it totally uninhabitable (if indeed any type of coherent world could have ever existed in such a universe to begin with).

However, there is another important reason why we could never live in this sort of energy-maximizing world. It has to do with the phenomenon of spiritual growth, and with our own contribution to this all-important process. For had we not been lazy by our very nature, our growth spurts would have essentially happened on their own, without any significant contribution from us. But this would have effectively removed us from any type of direct participation in our own development, which in turn would have had the devastating consequence of virtually eliminating any type of intimate relationship between our development and our innermost selves. And since the very nature of the Human Essence is presumably predicated upon just such an intimate relationship, in which the various human virtues are gradually developed through a hard-won deposit of personal energy and effort, we find that we could never have been genuinely human to begin with in such an entropy-reducing world. There is no way around it: we absolutely have to struggle for our own growth if we are to be fully human, because this is the only way that we can be truly in charge of our own development; otherwise, we would have grown more or less automatically towards our goal of individuation, and this, in turn, would have caused us to be mere spectators of our own development instead of active participants in it.

Job's Goodness and the Nature of Evil

Getting back to our Biblical story, we find that God is very proud of His servant Job, since he has persevered in his goodness in spite of the many calamities that have befallen him. "Have you considered my servant Job?" He asks Satan a second time. "There is no one on earth like him; he is blameless and upright, a man who fears God and shuns evil. And he still maintains his integrity, though you incited me against him to ruin him without any reason" (Job 2:3).

Here we learn that it is indeed the dark side of God who has brought ruin to Job's estate, and not Satan, because it explicitly says that Satan incited *God* against Job to ruin him without any reason. So it is clearly *God* who somehow brings about these destructive events upon Job, and not Satan. Satan simply tempts God into thinking that Job *might* sin if he loses his wealth and prosperity.

Satan thus seems to symbolically represent the ruthless testing action of life itself, which repeatedly subjects people to trials and tribulations in order to bring to light any evils that might be hidden inside of them. The purpose of this sort of "trial by fire" is to purify the individual as much as possible, but this can only happen when one is repeatedly subjected to pain and suffering, as we have seen. For just as impure iron ore must be repeatedly heated before it can yield pure iron, so too must the personality be repeatedly "heated" before it can rid itself of its own hidden impurities.

No one is immune from this kind of natural second-guessing by life itself, because we are all still tainted to one degree or another with a wide variety of inner psychospiritual impurities. While we may be perfectly "good" in terms of our day-to-day behavior, this isn't quite good enough for the kingdom of heaven, because God judges us in terms of our *inner* reality, not in terms of how well we behave on the outside, and the reason for this isn't far to seek: God wants us to be able to meet *any* kind of obstacle or stress without going wrong, because this is the only way we can be guaranteed not to sin in heaven. However, the only way we can achieve this goal is by becoming fully mature and developed on the inside. This is why being good on the outside isn't good enough for God: because in another set of circumstances we could easily become evil, and this would clearly jeopardize our long-term worthiness for the kingdom. So, unless we can be reasonably assured of not going wrong in *any* set of circumstances, we are not yet fit for the kingdom, because we have not yet been fully developed.

For instance, let us consider the life of a hypothetical man named Smith, who is a very "good" individual by just about anyone's criteria. He goes to church every Sunday, gives ten percent of his income to the poor, and is a great father and husband. At the same time, though, he is also blessed with good health, great wealth, and a general lack of any significant opposing force in his life.

On the face of it, Smith seems like a perfectly good guy. But suppose this very same individual happened to exist at the time of the Nazi occupation of Germany. Worse yet, suppose that these vastly altered circumstances were somehow able to capitalize on Smith's inner weaknesses in such a way that he would have become a ruthless Nazi executioner.

Now, given this new information, can we still properly call Smith good? Clearly not, even though he may have been perfectly well behaved in his real-world life. *For as far as the kingdom of heaven is concerned, it is of no laudable consequence that one is capable of being good in good circumstances, because this kind of behavior does not spring from the true quality of one's inner self; it springs instead from the goodness of one's surroundings. What ultimately matters is how one behaves in bad circumstances, because this is where the true quality of one's inner self is actually revealed.* And since God is primarily interested in well-developed human souls who are capable of being good in the most trying of circumstances, anything less will always be insufficient.

It doesn't matter that we only have only one life to be tested in at this point in our development, because we will presumably have the opportunity to grow and be tested in additional worlds beyond the grave. There are also many different sub-situations in our present life that serve the same purpose as being tested in an entirely different era. This is the function of all the trials and tribulations that we inevitably experience in our earthly lives: they test the true inner fabric of our souls, so as to determine what we are truly made of. If evil is revealed, it can then be brought out into the open, where it can be subsequently dealt with and resolved.

In this sense Satan can be thought of as the archetype of self-purification, which takes place through emotional fire and personal turmoil. His task is to make sure that each individual soul is as pure and well-developed as it is humanly possible to be, but in order to accomplish this feat, he must force each individual to contend with a wide variety of problems, including heart-wrenching calamities.

Given this highly ambitious job, it comes as no surprise that Satan isn't satisfied with the limited amount of destruction that he has wrought upon Job. How could he be? Since Job was by no means optimally developed from a psychospiritual point of view, it was necessary for him to be repeatedly tested and purified with fire in order for this desired end to be fully realized. This is why Satan rebukes God's praising of Job with the enigmatic saying "skin for skin" (Job 2:4), which means that as far as Satan (or the

Law of Natural Causation) is concerned, Job was willing to give up the skin of his children, servants, and livestock in order to preserve his own skin. This is clearly symbolic of how life always seems be reproaching and even mocking us in response to the Law of Natural Causation, which spares no one of even a single destructive effect in the world when the corresponding destructive causes are engaged in. Indeed, Satan goes on to raise the ante with God one step further by asserting that Job's goodness will disappear instantaneously if God strikes Job down with bodily torment (Job 2:5).

This is certainly a legitimate reproach as far as the vast majority of human beings are concerned, so it is understandable that Satan—acting as the very personification of the Law of Natural Causation—would assert to God that Job's goodness is literally only skin deep. And in actuality there is good reason for this belief; namely, that the true spiritual wickedness inside of most people is buried so deep that only the most profound forms of bodily torment are capable of revealing it. Being human, of course, this was undoubtedly true of Job to some extent, which explains why God felt compelled to go along with Satan's insidious request: because God is only satisfied with complete inner purity and developmental perfection, and He knows that being tried with fire is the best way to bring about these virtuous qualities in people.

We mustn't forget that God will spare no effort in trying to help us become fully developed on the inside, even if it means allowing us to suffer horrendous pain for a time, because He knows that this is the only way we'll ever be considered worthy enough to be adopted into His spiritual family.[13] Indeed, St. Paul tells us that the kingdom of heaven is anxiously awaiting the revealing of the sons of God (i.e., fully developed humans) at this moment in time. However, this can only happen *after* we humans have purified our innermost souls of their accumulated evils, because this is by far the most important prerequisite to our becoming fully mature and individuated on the inside. Unfortunately, though, this ambitious goal can only be realized through *extreme* emotional hardship and physical suffering, which is what the cross in Christian theology is meant to symbolize.

There is no question that Job had to face the pain of the cross in his own personal life, because he was quickly struck down with a severe skin disease when Satan was allowed to have his diabolical way with him:

> So Satan went out from the presence of the Lord and afflicted Job with painful sores from the soles of his feet to the top of his head. Then Job took a piece of broken pottery and scraped himself with it as he sat among the ashes.
>
> His wife said to him, "Are you still holding on to your integrity? Curse God and die!"

He replied, "You are talking like a foolish woman. Shall we accept good from God, and not trouble?"

In all this, Job did not sin in what he said (Job 2:7–10).

Notice how we're told that despite all his suffering, "Job did not sin in what he said" (Job 2:10). This is significant, because it leaves open the possibility that Job's sinlessness was confined primarily to his verbal behavior only. While it is possible that he was just as sinless on the inside as he was on the outside, it is also possible that he was literally "guilty as sin" on the inside, and that his verbal sinlessness did not accurately reflect the true state of his inner wickedness. Unfortunately, this is the way most people are at this point in our developmental journey, which gives us even *more* reason to suppose that Job wasn't yet a saint on the inside.

One of the most important things that we can learn from the book of Job is that no one on earth has yet attained to perfection in the sense of being fully developed or self-actualized.[14] None of us has yet been initiated into the full glory of the kingdom of God, so we are *all* liable to being tested and purified in the "fire of life" in the same way that Job was. No one is good enough to be exempt from this purifying process, not even a great man like Job, so we shouldn't be surprised to see good people routinely suffering throughout our world. Indeed, Job was the most righteous man in his entire country, yet God, working through the Principle of Natural Causation, found it necessary to test and purify him in order to make him fit for the kingdom. But most of us aren't nearly as good as Job was; therefore, we can reasonably expect to face *at least* as many trials and tribulations during our brief stay on this planet as Job did.

A fitting analogy to this cleansing process can be drawn to the construction of a bridge. If our goal is to construct a well-designed bridge, with no hairline cracks or weak spots, the only way we can be sure that we have achieved our goal is to rigorously test the bridge when it is completed. If any cracks or weak spots still exist within it, they will in all likelihood show up under the testing. And if and when they do in fact show up, they can then be subsequently identified and repaired in the interest of preserving the bridge's safety for humans. In the event that the bridge is found to possess huge underlying flaws, it might even have to be torn down completely so that it can be properly built anew.

The human personality is much the same way, except for one major difference. It is theoretically possible for a bridge to be built perfectly (or close to it) from the start, but it is *not* possible for a human soul to be built perfectly from the start in the same way. This is because the very definition of humanity seems to require that we be in control of our own development from essentially the very beginning of our lives. So, insofar as this is indeed the case, it is *inevitable* that we will grow up with major cracks and flaws in our personality, because the very essence of character immaturity is imperfection. Within this developmental context, the trials and tribulations of life function to put our personalities to the test, so that our internal flaws can subsequently be exposed and appropriately dealt with as necessary.

Of course, if our personalities could have been created ready-made to begin with, they would have never required such an interim process of self-purification in order to be fit for the kingdom. Unfortunately, the very essence of the Human Definition seems to require that the individual be capable of directing herself through the entire span of self-development from conception to full character assembly. This apparent necessity makes it inevitable that we will develop a large number of flaws within our character structure, as we have seen, which will then need to be cleansed by the many fires of life. These flaws are a direct consequence of our own partial character assembly, because anything that is as complex as the human personality cannot be expected to exist in a partially assembled state without severe problems resulting. The many psychological disorders to which the human mind is naturally subject are a lasting testimony to the tremendous disequilibrating power of this type of ontological problem.

It would be a mistake, however, to assume that God directly metes out trials and tribulations in the world in order to purify us. To the contrary, these evils seem to be a natural consequence of the way in which our world was originally set up. Insofar as this supposition is indeed accurate, God can only be held to be responsible for His original creation of the world, as we have seen, and not necessarily for every contingent act that subsequently takes place within it. This doesn't generally present a problem for most theists, however, who tend to believe that there is some important element of underlying necessity to the entire world order.

It would also be a mistake to assume that God is allowing Satan as an external agent to attack individual human beings who somehow deserve to be punished. We *all* deserve to suffer, yet many types of calamities seem to strike in an entirely random, and therefore unplanned, fashion. This observation makes it unlikely that either God or Satan is directly punishing people through the various acts of destruction in our world.

While the Bible may describe the origin of Job's suffering in terms of a conspiracy between God and Satan, this appears to be more of a literary device than it does a literal description of how evil comes about in the world. For to the extent that Satan is the personification of the Principle of Natural Causation in the world, and to the extent that this Principle is perpetually scanning the entire globe looking for flaws and vulnerabilities to attack, then this sort of naturalistic Satan can indeed be thought of as being "out there" causing trials and tribulations in human society, but *only* in response to the various character weaknesses and poor behavioral choices that we ourselves are guilty of.

This of course is a variation on the age-old Law of Karma, which states that our sufferings in this world are directly related to the inherent quality of our past actions. For the Hindus and certain other religious sects, the Law of Karma is believed to reach back to previous lives, so that our suffering in this world is considered to be a natural punishment for past evils that were committed in a former life. There is, however, no way to verify either the existence of past lives or the transworld linking of karmic punishment. But what we *can* do is trace our present-day experiences to our previous actions *in this world*. On this single world level the Law of Karma appears to be very true indeed, because it is a matter of common experience that we eventually get what's coming to us in our lives. Even the Bible agrees on this important point, because we're told in the book of Galatians that we will only end up reaping what we sow in this lifetime:

Be not deceived; God is not mocked: for whatsoever a man soweth, that shall he also reap. For he that soweth to his flesh shall of the flesh reap corruption; but he that soweth to the Spirit shall of the Spirit reap life everlasting (Gal. 6:7–8, KJV).

The point is simply that actions have consequences, *natural* consequences, and that these are the consequences that will either glorify us or punish us in the future.

As far as natural disasters like earthquakes, hurricanes, and tornadoes are concerned, these seem to be generated by physical vulnerabilities in the earth's geological and climatological makeup. As a consequence, there appears to be absolutely no connection between the occurrence of specific natural disasters and the wickedness of a given population, as we have seen. These types of disasters seem to strike randomly, but since we're all wicked to some extent, those who are caught in the middle of these disasters will subsequently have their wickedness directly put to the test.

On the other hand, there is a sense in which God *does* want us to suffer, not in any particular instance *per se*, but in general. He knows that we are full of inner defects and psychological barriers that are preventing our free forward movement towards our own full development, so He naturally wants us to become cleansed of these inner problems as quickly as possible.

At the same time, though, He knows that the very definition of our essence prevents Him from miraculously solving our problems for us. We have to solve our own developmental problems for ourselves before we can qualify as being genuinely human, so He naturally wants us to have those experiences in life that will facilitate this kind of psychospiritual progress. Unfortunately for us, these growth-facilitating events are almost always experienced in a negative, aversive manner.

This is the sense in which God has pre-arranged our suffering for us. He doesn't cause any specific evil events *per se*, as He seems to have done (albeit indirectly) in the book of Job. He simply has set the world up from the very beginning in such a way that evil events will naturally happen of their own accord. In this way God doesn't have to be burdened with the extraordinary problem of having to directly cause human suffering in the world; He can just "sit back," as it were, and allow the natural course of events to take place in our lives.

So, evil seems to be a necessary (though temporary) feature of human life on three separate counts. First, evil seems to be indispensable insofar as it is metaphysically necessary for humans to be partially developed at the present time (due to the specific demands of their underlying essence). This relation between evil and our own self-assembly is due to the fact that partial character development in and of itself seems to be responsible for most of the moral evil that takes place in our world, as we have seen.

This inner evil can be better understood mechanistically, in terms of an object that is in the process of getting assembled. Since no one in this world has yet become fully individuated, there is a very real sense in which our characters are only partially assembled at the present time.[15] It is this partial character assembly that is the proximate cause of moral evil, because all complex structures malfunction *by definition* when they are partially assembled.

This principle of optimal mechanical functioning is as true for mechanical devices as it is for human beings. Take a partially assembled automobile, for instance. If it is taken out on the road for a premature test drive, it is clearly going to malfunction as a direct consequence of its own partial assembly; and unfortunately, we human beings are precisely the same way, since we are also prone to behavioral malfunctioning as a direct consequence of our own partial character assembly. It is in this sense that human evil can be said to result from Murphy's Law. For insofar as it is true that anything that *can* go wrong *will* go wrong eventually, then it must also be true that the partially-developed human character structure must itself be prone to going wrong eventually as well, because it is in the very nature of partially-developed things to malfunction from time to time.

Unfortunately, we humans have no choice but to be partially assembled at the present time, because this is the only way that we can assemble ourselves, so to speak, through our own day-to-day behaviors in the world. It is this process of psychological self-assembly that makes us truly human in the larger Scheme of Things, as we have seen, because it gives us the freedom to determine who we really are and want to be in our lives. It also gives us genuine possession over our innermost thoughts and feelings as well, because the only way we can ever truly own anything in this life is to struggle for it through our own hard effort.

We have also seen how this phenomenon of partial character assembly in human beings is itself comprised of two principal components: an epistemological component and a moral component. The epistemological component is comprised of a pervasive lack of practical knowledge about how to go about doing the good, while the moral component derives its essence from an inner unwillingness to do what is right in all possible circumstances. Taken together, these two components are very efficient in bringing about moral evil in the world, for as long as our characters are not fully assembled, we either won't be knowledgeable enough to prevent evil in our lives, or else we won't morally want to, or both.

The second way in which evil seems to be a necessary (though again temporary) feature of human life has to do with its purgative effect on the inner self. For insofar as it is inevitable that human beings will become bogged down in their developmental journey by any number of different psychological barriers, a way must be found for these problems to be expunged from the personality. And as it turns out, the most effective and efficient purgative force in the world is the internal suffering that is caused by pain.

An appropriate analogy for this relationship between pain and self-purification can be found in the field of surgery. Everyone recognizes that the single most effective way to remove a cancerous tumor from the body is through the pain and suffering caused by a surgeon's knife. However, the same basic principle can also be seen to apply to our own psychospiritual development as well, because an analogous form of pain and suffering, induced by the force of evil in the world, is by far the most effective way of removing the various psychopathologies from our personality.

Indeed, this is the ultimate meaning of the cross in Christian theology. Jesus' crucifixion is directly symbolic of the inner "crucifixion" that we *all* must undergo before we can be cleansed of the many growth-inhibiting hang-ups that we have accumulated throughout our lives. Jesus' resurrection from the dead is thus symbolic of the new psychospiritual life that we will naturally be born into when we finally become fully individuated.

Evil is also necessary in human affairs because it is one of the most potent facilitators of spiritual growth in existence. This is especially true when it comes to the difficult task of becoming more conscious in our lives, as John Sanford explains in the following passage:

> Fulfillment can only come when the conscious personality expresses in a unified life as completely as possible the totality of the personality, most of which, to begin with, is unknown to us.
>
> For this to happen, all the various parts of us must perform their proper function, and the proper function of the ego includes becoming conscious, that is, psychologically enlightened and aware. But the ego is a sleepy bear who prefers to hibernate. Few people become conscious without *having*

to become conscious, without being driven to it by necessity. And this is where evil comes in. For the most part, it is only when people encounter evil in some form—as pain, loss of meaning, or something that appears to be threatening or destructive to them—that they begin to find their way to consciousness. And only when people are tested in the fire of life, so that what is weak within them is purged away and only the strong elements remain, does individuation take place. This purging can only take place in the context of a certain amount of suffering and struggle. Paradoxically, without a power in life that seems to oppose wholeness, the achievement of wholeness would be impossible. From the point of view of psychology, evil is a necessity if individuation is to occur.[16]

This surprising conclusion raises an even deeper question: if evil is a necessary (though again temporary) feature of human life, can it properly be called evil in the end? This is an intriguing question that seems to have two separate answers. On the one hand, there does indeed seem to be a possible sense in which most evils will turn out to be good in the long run, but *only* on the precondition that evil is somehow metaphysically necessary in an instrumental sense for the attainment of the greatest possible good for humanity.[17] On the other hand, when evil is experienced in the here-and-now by suffering humans, it is unquestionably evil. *It is thus only from the largest possible perspective that evil could possibly turn out to be good in the future.* This view harks back to Augustine's aesthetic view of evil, which asserts that evil is similar to the dark splotches in a painting. Both seem pointless and even ugly when viewed by themselves, but this quality instantly vanishes when these isolated items are viewed from a larger holistic perspective.

However, even this aesthetic view seems to be contradicted by the sheer amount of catastrophic evil in the world. While some form of evil may be necessary for the existence and development of human beings, it is difficult to see why there must be so much of it, or why it must frequently be so cataclysmic. This is the problem of *dysteleological* evil in its purest form.

Two answers can be given to this problem. To begin with, the very existence of partially-developed human souls seems to naturally bring with it an extreme amount of pain and evil. In this sense, partially-developed human existence is like war: neither can exist without causing a tremendous amount of suffering and destructiveness.

This conclusion can most clearly be seen with moral evil, because ignorant and morally immature free agents can readily be expected to produce a wide variety of catastrophic evils with their behavior. However, natural evils can also be shown to be part of the whole character-building scheme as well, as Swinburne and Reichenbach have so aptly pointed out.[18] Unfortunately, space limitations require that I put off further inquiry into this matter to a later work.[19]

A second possible function for *prima facie* dysteleological evil can be seen to be related to the necessary conditions for our own psychospiritual transformation. It is a well-known fact that most of the psychological barriers that we harbor deep inside are *extremely* tenacious; so much so, in fact, that they can only be uprooted and eliminated by a force that is *equally* efficacious. Unfortunately, it appears as though nothing less than genuinely catastrophic suffering will work in this capacity. For just as a surgeon's scalpel must be sharp enough to cut through the different layers of bodily tissue so that a cancerous tumor can be isolated and removed, so too must the evils in our lives be "sharp" enough to cut through all of our deeply embedded psychological defenses.[20]

The evidence from our day-to-day lives bears out this conclusion. For better or for worse, most people never change in any significant fashion in their lives. While they may undergo a large number of career and lifestyle changes, the orientation of their inner minds rarely, if ever, changes. Thus, most people who are cruel and hateful at age twenty will in all likelihood remain cruel and hateful at age sixty. Of course, there are notable exceptions to this observation, but by and large we all seem to be locked into the various character traits that we in fact possess.

Indeed, it would seem that the only people who are capable of experiencing a significant amount of inner change are those who have been exposed to some form of catastrophic evil. Time and time again we hear about people whose lives have been utterly changed by an inadvertent experience of profound suffering. The overwhelming power of this kind of inner torment seems to have a healing and transforming effect on the personality, and the amount of transformation that takes place seems to be directly proportional to the degree of evil that has been experienced, at least to a point. Beyond this point, of course, catastrophic evil either maims or kills outright, but even when it does, it remains possible for a beneficial developmental effect to ultimately be realized beyond the grave.

Again, this appears to be the primary meaning of the cross in human life. Jesus didn't die an easy, pain-free death when He was crucified. To the contrary, He died one of the most excruciating[21] and horrible deaths imaginable, and according to St. Peter, we're supposed to do the same sort of thing in our own lives, because "Christ also suffered for us, leaving us an example, that [we] should follow in his steps" (1 Pet. 2:21). This doesn't mean, however, that we literally need to be crucified to a cross before we can be redeemed. It simply means that we need to find a way to "crucify" our inner developmental barriers so they can be eliminated once and for all. More often than not, this means being exposed to some type of horrendous evil.

The Christian ritual of communion fits in perfectly with this idea. For what other practical function could possibly be served by the symbolic consumption of Christ's body and blood during communion, apart from the literal incorporation of His profound suffering within our own lives? That is to say, the larger purpose of communion seems to be to symbolically prepare us for the same sort of literal suffering that Jesus experienced on the cross. This explains why we are supposed to symbolically consume his body and blood: because we are *literally* supposed to suffer our way to salvation in the same general way He did, since this is apparently the only way there is for us to effectively defuse the many developmental barriers within us that are blocking our way to individuation.

Most writers on the theodicy question, however, have failed to take these inner psychospiritual barriers seriously enough, and this has caused their resulting theodicies to be out of focus. The truth of the matter is that these barriers aren't simply lodged inside of our minds; *they are intimately intertwined within the very fabric of our innermost souls*. This is why their removal requires such a truly heroic effort before it can be successful: because it necessitates the forceful unwinding of our *entire* psychological makeup. This explains why it is so hard to do, and why only catastrophic evils are typically able to accomplish the task.

Of course, one person's mild setback is another person's catastrophic evil. Thus, the subjective experience of evil is a relative matter, such that the very same event might have a catastrophic (and therefore purgative) effect on one person, while on another it might not have much effect at all. What is required, then, is the *subjective* experience of catastrophic suffering before a given event can be considered to be truly purgative. Indeed, patients in Arthur Janov's Primal Therapy Clinic don't experience any type of external evil at all in the present, yet they often suffer more than enough to be purged of their inner repressions, because they are getting in touch with their *past* emotional traumas, which are lodged deep inside their unconscious.

It is for this reason we can say that the chief function of catastrophic evil in the purgative process is merely to break down our defensive external front so that our entire repressed side can be given free access into consciousness, where it can then be reintegrated into the whole personality. Unfortunately, this process of reintegration will rarely, if ever, happen on its own. Rather, it typically has to be forced upon us by some type of external evil before it will take place, which explains Jesus' enigmatic saying that He didn't come to bring peace on the earth but a sword (Matt. 10:34). It also explains why the kingdom of God is typically ushered into the personality through some type of catastrophic experience.

John Sanford agrees:

> It is those who have recognized that they have been injured or hurt in some way in life who are most apt to come into the kingdom. There is no

virtue in our weakness or injury as such, especially if this leads to self-pity, which completely defeats the creative purposes of the kingdom. But only a person who has recognized his or her own need, even despair, is ready for the kingdom; those who feel they are self-sufficient, those whom life has upheld in their one-sided orientation, remain caught in their egocentricity.

This is why Jesus so often associated with sinners and tax collectors and was generally unable to have a relationship with the Pharisees, for the latter, as a rule, were upheld in their egocentricity by their privileged position in society and by their conviction of their own righteousness. But sinners and tax collectors, if they turned and confronted themselves, could be receptive to the kingdom. . . .

It is because of the demanding nature of the kingdom that our entrance into it frequently puts us in a crisis. . . . All of the old person and all the old attitudes are challenged by the kingdom. Our response to this challenge is crucial and determines whether we will go the way of creativity or the way of unconsciousness. This is the "ego-crisis," a time of judgment but also of opportunity. It is in this light that the sense of urgency regarding the kingdom, of which Jesus frequently speaks, is to be understood. The time is fulfilled, and humanity is now to respond; the consequences of turning aside the kingdom cannot be avoided, nor can we postpone our response any longer.[22]

Now we are in a position to understand Jesus' enigmatic saying that everyone is getting into the kingdom through violence (Luke 16:16). The mere concept of violence, of course, implies an inner intensity of experience that is the very hallmark of genuine spiritual growth, and it is precisely this sort of inner development that will eventually enable us to enter the kingdom. A similar motif underlies the Parable of the Wedding Feast, in which Jesus compares the kingdom of heaven to a man who was preparing a great feast for his son:

"At the time of the banquet he sent his servant to tell those who had been invited, 'Come, for everything is now ready.'

"But they all alike began to make excuses. The first said, 'I have just bought a field, and I must go and see it. Please excuse me.' Another said, 'I have just bought five yoke of oxen, and I'm on my way to try them out. Please excuse me.' Still another said, 'I just got married, so I can't come.'

"The servant came back and reported this to his master. Then the owner of the house became angry and ordered his servant, 'Go out quickly into the streets and alleys of the town and bring in the poor, the crippled, the blind and the lame.'

"'Sir,' the servant said, 'what you ordered has been done, but there is still room.' Then the master told his servant, 'Go out to the roads and country lanes and make them come in, so that my house will be full. I tell you, not one of those men who were invited will get a taste of my banquet'" (Luke 14:16–24).

Those who had initially been invited to the feast proved to be unworthy because they were too preoccupied with their own egocentric concerns to be able to spare the time to attend. This is why it is the poor, the blind, and the lame who end up coming to the great feast instead: because they are the only ones who aren't so caught up in their own materialistic lives that they can't devote themselves to other things.

This paradoxical principle also applies directly to our entrance into the kingdom of God as well, because the more privileged members of society will almost certainly turn out to be too preoccupied with their own worldly concerns to be able to seriously attend to higher spiritual matters. This explains why it is so hard for the rich to enter the kingdom of heaven (Matt. 19:24), and why many of the first in this lifetime will allegedly be the last in the next world, and vice versa (Matt. 20:16): because material self-sufficiency in this world almost invariably causes one to neglect the higher spiritual concerns of the kingdom. This problem, of course, doesn't generally affect the poor and the infirm, who also possess the added advantage of suffering a great deal in their day-to-day lives. Together, these two factors make it *much* more likely that the poor and the downtrodden of this world will be among the first to enter the kingdom, because they are the ones who are most likely to suffer in the same catastrophic sense that the kingdom seems to require.

There is no doubt that Job's many consecutive losses caused him to suffer in this horrible catastrophic sense. For not only did he lose his children, servants, and livestock in the span of just a few minutes, he also lost his physical health in a way few of us can imagine. Ryrie[23] has suggested that Job may have been suffering from some form of elephantiasis or leukemia of the skin, since the entire surface of his body was afflicted with painful sores that itched him intensely. His condition was so bad that his skin became hard and crusty and even attracted worms (Job 7:5). What could be worse than this?

Indeed, when Job's three friends, Eliphaz, Bildad, and Zophar, came to visit him, they were so taken aback by his horrible suffering that they were unable to say a word to him for a week. Instead, they sat silently with him for seven consecutive days and nights in a continuous vigil of heartfelt friendship.

To his supreme credit, Job was able to maintain his personal integrity throughout this entire period of time. Finally, though, he gave in to his profound inner torment and cursed the day of his birth:

"May the day of my birth perish, and the night it was said, 'A boy is born!' That day—may it turn to darkness; may God above not care about it; may no light shine upon it.

May darkness and deep Shadow claim it once more; may a cloud settle over it; may blackness overwhelm its light. That night—may thick darkness seize it; may it not be included among the days of the year nor be entered in any of the months. May that night be barren; may no shout of joy be heard in it. May those who curse days curse that day, those who are ready to rouse Leviathan. May its morning stars become dark; may it wait for daylight in vain and not see the first rays of dawn, for it did not shut the doors of the womb on me to hide trouble from my eyes.

Why did I not perish at birth, and die as I came from the womb?

Why were there knees to receive me and breasts that I might be nursed? For now I would be lying down in peace; I would be asleep and at rest with kings and counselors of the earth, who built for themselves places now lying in ruins, with rulers who had gold, who filled their houses with silver. Or why was I not hidden in the ground like a stillborn child, like an infant who never saw the light of day? There the wicked cease from turmoil, and there the weary are at rest. Captives also enjoy their ease; they no longer hear the slave driver's shout.

The small and the great are there, and the slave is freed from his master. Why is light given to those in misery, and life to the bitter of soul, to those who long for death that does not come, who search for it more than for hidden treasure, who are filled with gladness and rejoice when they reach the grave?

Why is life given to a man whose way is hidden, whom God has hedged in? For sighing comes to me instead of food; my groans pour out like water. What I feared has come upon me; what I dreaded has happened to me. I have no peace, no quietness; I have no rest, but only turmoil" (Job 3:3–26).

More poetic renditions of personal torment have probably never been written. Job's profound anguish is described so well that his pain seems to leap off the printed page and into the reader's exasperated mind.

It is interesting to note Job's claim that his primary fear and dread has finally come upon him (Job 3:25). There are two ways we can understand this. On the one hand, we can take it at face value, and simply assume that Job has long feared this kind of bodily incapacitation for obvious reasons. On the other hand, we can take it on a deeper, more psychological level. For if Job's external sores can be taken to represent the internal repressions that we all have hidden away deep inside of us, then his long-standing fear of this kind of bodily illness could symbolically represent *every* individual's fear of the inner Shadow.

Indeed, this is why we repress our most painful feelings to begin with: because we fear them with a vengeance. Once we repress them, though, we force ourselves to live in perpetual fear and dread of them for the rest of our lives. And moreover, while we may not consciously be aware of the true nature of our inner fears, this doesn't reduce their horrendous impact upon our lives one iota.

On an unconscious level, then, our greatest fear is that our unconscious repressions will suddenly spring forward upon us when we least expect it. It is our greatest fear because our entire character structure has been organized around these subterranean pains and anxieties, as Ernest Becker has so aptly pointed out.[24] This is why our greatest fear will indeed come upon us one day in the future: because our repressions will eventually be liberated into consciousness, either in this lifetime or in the Afterlife, because it is the single greatest precondition for our future wholeness.

The Nature of Hell

Indeed, the Biblical experience of hell may actually turn out to be directly related to the spontaneous release of our repressions upon our physical death. Jesus Himself tells us in Matt. 8:12 that there will be weeping, wailing, and gnashing of teeth in hell, and not coincidentally, this is exactly what people do when they are forced to confront and feel their own repressions *en masse.*

This view is supported by an intriguing passage from the Gospel of Luke, where Jesus tells us that "there is nothing concealed that will not be disclosed, or hidden that will not be made known" (Luke 12:3). This saying perfectly describes the frightening process of unrepression, in which the mind's many repressions suddenly flood the conscious ego with an entire lifetime of unwanted pains and fears. On this view, it isn't physical fire that the Bible is referring to when it speaks of hell; it is *emotional* "fire," which describes very nicely what is known to be experienced when our unconscious repressions are suddenly released into consciousness.

According to *The Tibetan Book of the Dead*, this is precisely what will happen to us upon our physical death. For once we are suddenly deprived of our cognitive physiological environment with its attendant defense mechanisms upon our bodily demise, we will temporarily enter a transition period known as the *bardo state*, in which we will automatically manufacture, through the psychic process of projection, an "external" reality that will directly reflect the inner psychological reality that we have been building up for ourselves during our life on earth. If we have cleansed ourselves of most of our inner repressions in our previous life, then we will automatically manufacture for ourselves a pleasant, and even heavenly, state of mind. If, on the other hand, we have accumulated a significant backlog of unconscious repressions during our earthly lives, these repressions will then be liberated in full force upon our physical death, and this will be experienced as hell in the most literal sense of the word.[25]

John Hick has written an excellent description of this bardo or interim state in *Death and Eternal Life*. He begins by postulating that it may indeed be possible, upon our physical death, for us to enter the "final self-transcending perfection" that we are all ultimately intended for. However,

. . . in the great majority of cases we are not able to face Ultimate Reality, or even to be conscious that it confronts us, and so we continue our individual ego-existences. In that case we regain consciousness in a post-mortem state which, according to the indications both of the *Bardo Thödol* and of western mediumistic communications, is subjective or dream-like. As such it is an experience through which the individual encounters aspects of his own total self, including its unconscious depths, of which he was not directly aware in his waking life on earth. This is an experience of self-discovery and of the realization of what one has become through the good and bad choices, the brave facings of difficulties and the cowardly turnings away from them, the self-givings and the refusals to give, the generosities and selfishnesses, the impulsive acts of creation and of destruction, and all the varied cumulative thoughts, emotions, intentions, hopes and fears and dreams—beautiful and ugly, healthy and vicious, splendid and contemptible, humane and fiendish—which have been continuously modifying our conscious and unconscious nature between birth and death. This gradually formed psychic structure is, in eastern terms, our karma. It is what we have become in the course of what we have done. And in the first phase of existence after death, as the ego is freed from the constraints of the physical world, this karma . . . makes itself known to us in experiences both of wish-fulfillment and self-judgement. . . . The 'realistic dreams' in which it consists may take many different forms, depending largely upon the beliefs and the consequent anticipations of different individuals. We should accordingly expect any echoes from the next world, received by some kind of extra-sensory awareness, to vary considerably from culture to culture. The *Bardo Thödol* describes the post-mortem experiences of a devout Tibetan Buddhist, in which, having shrunk from the Clear Light of Ultimate Reality, he encounters a series of benevolent deities who offer him salvation in their various realms of bliss. But if the good within him, which would respond to these invitations, is not sufficiently powerful to carry him into these worlds, then he goes on to encounter wrathful deities who represent the evil within him. As the *Bardo Thödol* makes clear, these beneficent and wrathful deities are all projections of his own mind. . . . On the other hand a devout Christian . . . would have had a quite different post-mortem experience. His coming to self-awareness would have taken the form of a divine judgement formed largely out of materials provided by the New Testament—a great assize in the presence of throngs of angels, saints, and martyrs, presided over either by the towering figure of God the Father seated on a great white throne and shining in an unapproachable light, or alternatively by Christ, the Lamb of God, seated on a throne and surrounded by his apostles. There might be angels reading from the Book of Life. And from this divine judgement he would proceed towards something which he would anticipate under the imagery of heaven or purgatory or hell. His expectations might then create for him a period of blissful or painful experiences according to the pattern of his beliefs.[26]

But it isn't merely the pattern of our expectations and beliefs that will help to determine the exact nature of our post-mortem experiences. Much more important in this capacity is the spiritual state of our innermost soul, or more precisely, the degree to which we have accumulated either good or bad memories and feelings within our unconscious. Accordingly, if we have failed to cleanse ourselves of most of the inner evils that we have accumulated for a lifetime, we will naturally project an external reality that is essentially unpleasant, and perhaps even hellish.

A particularly chilling description of this hellish bardo state is given in *The Tibetan Book of the Dead*:

"Oh son of noble family, at this time the great tornado of karma, terrifying, unbearable, whirling fiercely, will drive you from behind. Do not be afraid of it; it is your own confused projection. Dense darkness, terrifying and unbearable, will go before you, with terrible cries of 'Strike!' and 'Kill!' Do not be afraid of them. In the case of others who have done great evil, many flesh-eating demons will appear as a result of their karma, bearing various weapons, yelling warcries, shouting 'Kill! Strike!' and so on. You will feel that you are being chased by various terrifying wild animals and pursued by a great army in snow, rain, storms and darkness. There will be sounds of mountains crumbling, of lakes flooding of fire spreading, and of fierce winds springing up. In fear you will escape wherever you can, but you will be cut off by three precipices in front of you, white, red and black, deep and dreadful, and you will be on the point of falling down them.

"O son of noble family, they are not really precipices, they are aggression, passion and ignorance. . . . It is your own karma, that you are suffering like this, so you cannot blame anyone else. It is your own karma, so now supplicate the Three Jewels fervently, they will protect you. If you do not supplicate like this, and do not know the Great Symbol meditation, and do not meditate on your yidam, then the good conscience within you will collect all your good actions and count out white pebbles, and the bad conscience within you will collect all your evil actions and count out black pebbles. At this time you will be very frightened and terrified, and you will tremble and lie, saying, 'I have not sinned.' Then the Lord of Death will say, 'I will look in the mirror of karma,' and when he looks in the mirror all your sins and virtues will suddenly appear in it clearly and distinctly, so although you have lied it is of no use. Then the Lord of Death will drag you by a rope tied round your neck, and cut off your head, tear out your heart, pull out your entrails, lick your brains, drink your blood, eat your flesh and gnaw your bones; but you cannot die, so even though your body is cut into pieces you will recover.

"Being cut again and again causes extreme pain, so do not be afraid when the white pebbles are being counted, do not lie and do not fear the Lord of Death. Since you are a mental body you cannot die even if you are killed and cut up. You are really the natural form of emptiness, so there is no need to fear. The Lords of Death are the natural form of emptiness, your own confused projections, and you are emptiness, a mental body of unconscious tendencies. Emptiness cannot harm emptiness, the uncharacterised cannot harm the uncharacterised. External Lords of Death, gods, evil spirits, the Bull-headed demon and so on, have no reality apart from your own confused projections, so recognise this. At this moment recognise everything as the bardo."[27]

Our subjective level of suffering during this period will be greatly compounded by the simultaneous flooding of our conscious minds by our former repressions. In one fell swoop we will be forced to reexperience all the pains and fears that have been repressed within us for an entire lifetime, and the result will be nothing less than a genuine subjective hell.

Now, if this is indeed what the Biblical reality of hell is all about, then our self-confinement in this hellish realm of torment will probably be restricted to the time it takes to experience and resolve these inner repressions. If we are able to do this successfully, there doesn't seem to be any pressing reason for us to remain in hell any longer. One of Jesus' most cryptic sayings, which we encountered earlier, seems to make this very point:

Settle matters quickly with your adversary who is taking you to court. Do it while you are still with him on the way, or he may hand you over to the judge, and the judge may hand you over to the officer, and you may be thrown into prison. I tell you the truth, you will not get out until you have paid the last penny (Matt. 5:25–26).

As John Sanford[28] points out in *The Kingdom Within*, there are two possible levels of interpretation for this parable: an outer, sociological level, and an inner, psychological one. Taken on an outer level, Jesus' advice may be noteworthy, but it is hardly brilliant. It might also not be appropriate in all instances, either, since there are clearly times in which one should go all the way to court with one's opponent.

Taken on an inner, psychological level, though, Jesus' advice makes perfect sense. He is telling us that we need to come to terms with the psychospiritual adversary *within us* as soon as we possibly can, because if we don't, we will be held responsible for our divisive behavior by the court of the inner Self. And while part of this self-inflicted punishment may karmically happen to us in this world, most of it will probably happen in the next world, when the continued existence of our repressions will cause the inner Self to throw us into the psychological "prison" of profound emotional torment, as *The Tibetan Book of the Dead* astutely predicts. It is here that we will be given the task of having to face and re-integrate each of our repressions into the matrix of our overall personality. Once this process has begun, it is clear that we won't be able to get out of this self-inflicted hell until we have paid "the last penny," or until we have felt and re-integrated each and every one of our unconscious repressions.

This is both good news and bad news for those who want to know what the future holds in store for us. It is good news because it means that no one will be consigned to hell for eternity in opposition to their will. It is bad news, though, because it means that just about all of us will have to go through a temporary cleansing period in which our repressed pains will be purged from our innermost souls. This period corresponds roughly to the Purgatory of traditional Catholic theology.

This doctrine of eventual salvation for everyone is known as *universalism*. Although many people have argued persuasively for universalism over the years, this optimistic doctrine finds its best defense in John Hick's *Death and Eternal Life*.[29] Hick believes that the ultimate measure of success (and hence the absolute moral justifiability) of God's teleological goal for humankind will be severely compromised by the eternal loss of even a few souls; so much so, in fact, that the moral adequacy of God's ultimate accomplishment in this case could very well end up falling far short of that which is necessary to justify all of the evils that have taken place on this planet. As a consequence, Hick believes that God's eschatological goal will be perfect, and therefore ultimately untarnished, which in turn requires the eventual salvation of all human souls.

Hick is also opposed to the prospect of an eternal punishment in hell because he believes that it would be morally pointless, since it could never be utilized in the service of a higher good (at least not with respect to the lives of the eternally lost). Indeed, Hick asserts that an eternity of suffering in hell would establish good and evil as co-ordinates, which in turn would cause God's creation to be:

> . . . perpetually shadowed and spoiled by evil; and this would be incompatible either with God's sovereignty or with His perfect goodness. For the doctrine of hell has as its implied premise either that God does not desire to save all His human creatures, in which case He is only limitedly good, or that His purpose has finally failed in the case of some—and indeed, according to theological tradition, most—of them, in which case He is only limitedly sovereign. I therefore believe that the needs of Christian theodicy compel us to repudiate the idea of eternal punishment.[30]

Hick finds yet another objection to the idea of eternal damnation in hell in the infinite disproportion between finite human wrongdoing and infinite punishment, "for the absolute contrast of heaven and hell, entered immediately after death, does not correspond to the innumerable gradations of human good and evil; justice could never demand for finite human sins the infinite penalty of eternal pain; such unending torment could never serve any positive or reformative purpose precisely because it never ends."[31] This is an intriguing argument that seems to legislate decisively against any prospect of an eternal hell after the grave.

Indeed, Hick goes so far as to claim that any guarantee of a perfect moral outcome in the future for everyone is compatible with both human freedom *and* Divine omnipotence. He can say this because he believes, in sympathy with St. Augustine, that:

> God has made us for Himself, and our whole being seeks its fulfillment in relation to Him. He can influence us both through the world without and by the activity of His Holy Spirit within us, though always in ways that preserve the integrity and freedom of the human spirit. It seems morally (although still not logically) impossible that the infinite resourcefulness of infinite love working in unlimited time should be eternally frustrated, and the creature reject its own good, presented to it in an endless range of ways. We cannot say in advance *how* God will eventually free all created souls from their bondage to sin and establish them in love and glad obedience towards Himself; but despite the logical possibility of failure the probability of His success amounts, as it seems to me, to a practical certainty.[32]

Many fundamentalist Christians are opposed to the doctrine of universalism on Biblical grounds. They believe that the Bible clearly argues for an eternal hell for the damned. The fact is, though, that there are at least as many verses in the Bible that support universalism as those that support an eternal hell. For instance, the Bible tells us that God wills *all* to be saved; not a few, or even most, but *all* (1 Tim. 2:4). Now, if God wills *all* to be saved, then the only way to affirm the existence of an eternal hell is to conclude that God cannot accomplish His Will in the universe. This is an unacceptable conclusion for an omnipotent Creator, even if we accept the existence of radical freedom in humans, because one would think that a truly omnipotent Being would be able to *eventually* accomplish His ultimate Will in the universe, no matter what we humans may temporarily choose to the contrary. This is especially true if God has designed us for Him, so that our hearts will forever remain restless until they find their rest in Him. Eternity is, after all, an extremely long "time" for God's Will to be thwarted by His creation. Moreover, there is every reason to believe that even the most ignorant of human souls will eventually choose God-inspired life over an eternity of pain and suffering in hell; it may take trillions of years, but it seems very likely that it will eventually happen.

The Parable of the Lost Sheep supports this universalist conclusion:

> What do you think? If a man owns a hundred sheep, and one of them wanders away, will he not leave the ninety-nine on the hills and go to look for the one that wandered off? And if he finds it, I tell you the truth, he is happier about that one sheep than about the ninety-nine that did not wander off. In the same way your Father in heaven is not willing that any of these little ones should be lost (Matt. 18:12–14).

As far as the book of Revelation's eternal Lake of Fire is concerned, there is no compelling reason to believe that any human souls will actually be cast into it forever. While their evil *qualities* may be cast into it for eternity, it doesn't follow from this that the human owners of these qualities *themselves* will also be irrevocably cast into it. The book of Revelation only says that the devil and the false prophet will *definitely* be thrown into the Lake of Fire (Rev. 20:10). It doesn't say that any humans will *definitely* be thrown into it; only that those whose names aren't written in the Book of Life will be thrown in (Rev. 20:15). While this may be a true statement, it doesn't necessarily follow from this that anyone will *actually* be thrown into this Lake of Endless Torment, because it is a distinct possibility that everyone's names will eventually be written in the Book of Life.

As Hick and others have skillfully pointed out, universalism is the only fitting doctrine for a perfectly good, loving, and all-powerful Creator. We simply cannot expect anything less of Him, because an all-loving Deity would be compelled by definition to include everyone's name in the Book of Life if such a thing were even remotely possible. This conclusion remains valid even if it is ultimately up to each individual alone whether or not his or her name gets written into the Book of Life, because one would naturally expect God to have originally set the universe up in such a way as to make this choice a free-willed inevitability in the long run. Indeed, this was precisely the position that was held by St. Augustine, who believed, as we have seen, that God had slanted the nature of the human heart irrevocably toward Him.

A Developmental View of Salvation

It is interesting to note along the same lines that the apostle John, writing in the book of Revelation, asserted that we will all eventually be judged according to our actions in this world:

> And I saw the dead, great and small, standing before the throne, and the books were opened. Another book was opened, which is the book of life.

The dead were judged according to what they had done as recorded in the books. The sea gave up the dead that were in it, and death and Hades gave up the dead that were in them, and each person was judged according to what he had done (Rev. 20:12–13).

This view is consistent with the developmental view of salvation that has been put forth by Hick, Sanford, and others. For as long as we all must necessarily be given full control over our own development in order to be fully human, and as long as our entrance into the kingdom of God is contingent upon our attaining full character development, and finally, as long as the Divine process of judgment is an entirely natural cause and effect process, in which the psychospiritual causes in our lives will automatically be rewarded with their corresponding logical effects, then it follows that we will ultimately be judged according to our own actions in this world, because these are the events that will either facilitate or impair our actual entrance into the kingdom (*via* their natural effect on the individuating process itself).

The Bible tells us that each and every one of our behaviors is recorded in the Book of Life (Rev. 20:12). The "Book of Life," of course, is the "book" of our innermost souls. It "records" all of our behaviors in the sense that it immediately registers the natural (i.e., karmic) effect of our actions on the fabric of our overall personality. Thus, if a given behavior is positive and well-intentioned, it will automatically improve the quality (i.e., developmental maturity) of the personality, and this higher quality will automatically be "judged" by the Law of Cause and Effect in a positive manner, insofar as it will tend to cause primarily good things to happen in an individual's life. By contrast, if a given behavior is negative and maliciously intended, it will automatically detract from the intrinsic quality of the personality, and this diminished nature will tend to be "judged" in a negative manner by the Law of Cause and Effect. This in turn will tend to cause the individual to experience unpleasant consequences as a result.[33]

These self-imposed effects upon the personality, in turn, are naturally able to build upon themselves in classic "compound interest" style, so that after an entire lifetime, the personality will either end up being strong and healthy, weak and pathological, or somewhere in between, and all in response to how the individual actually behaved in his or her lifetime. This is undoubtedly why the major religions of the world emphasize good behavior so strongly: because it is our day-to-day behavior that has the predominant effect on how our personalities will turn out in the end. Thus, if our behavior has been good and well-intentioned over the years, we will naturally end up being "saved," because our well-developed souls will automatically make us fit for the kingdom. On the other hand, if our behavior has primarily been malicious throughout our lives, we will not be fit for the kingdom when we die, because our innermost personality will have self-developed into a sick and reprehensible entity.

This explains why immature and irresponsible people won't be allowed (by the natural perceptual system of the personality) into the kingdom of heaven: because it clearly wouldn't *be* heaven if people were going around doing evil things to one another. But hardly anyone ever becomes fully developed or individuated in this lifetime, so this seems to necessitate a developmental period beyond the grave in which we will be able to continue growing towards our ultimate psychospiritual goal. Many sincere Christians try to bypass this need for a self-obtained state of developmental perfection in the next life through the belief that God will instantaneously perfect us upon our death if we really and truly believe in Him. The problem with this scenario is that if God were going to instantaneously make us perfect after we die so that we can be fit for the kingdom, then He should have done so from the very beginning, and thereby enabled us to avoid all the evil of the present age. But He clearly hasn't done this, so we have little choice but to believe that such a thing is either metaphysically impossible, or else not in our best interest. Either way, *we* end up being primarily responsible for our own inner development, and hence for our ultimate acceptability into the kingdom.

Furthermore, there is no compelling reason to believe that our entrance into the kingdom will be controlled by an external, gate-like force. To the contrary, it seems as though it will most likely be mediated by our own state of psychospiritual development, so that if we are internally fit for the kingdom, we will *automatically* gain entry into it through a natural, self-mediated process upon our physical death. This position is supported by the popular contention that heaven is a state of mind much more than it is a concrete place. To the extent that this is indeed the case, our subjective experiences when we die will first and foremost be determined by our inner state of mind, just as *The Tibetan Book of the Dead* so emphatically points out.

Indeed, it is even possible that heaven and hell could end up being in the very same spiritual "place," since our subjective experience is so strongly determined by our inner state of mind, and not so much by where we happen to be existing at any given moment. We know this to be the case from our own psychological experience in this world, since it is a well known fact that two people can be in the same geographical place, and yet one can be in an inner "heaven," while the other can be in an inner "hell." Thus, the rich man in the Parable of Lazarus who is suffering in hell needn't be situated at a great geographical distance from Lazarus, who is in Paradise. Rather, the "great gulf" that is said to separate the two can actually be a *developmental* gulf, which could conceivably be made up of the tremendous ontological distance that naturally separates a healthy, well-developed person from a sick and depraved one.

It is important to understand, however, that this link between personal salvation and our individual behavior in the world is *not* at odds with the Biblical doctrine of salvation by faith, as many would like to believe. The crucial distinction that needs to be made here is between *salvation by faith* and *sanctification by works*. We are saved by faith because it is our faith in God's Developmental Plan for our lives that channels all of our subsequent behaviors towards the proper goal, which, once again, is our own full character development. At this point our partially developed existence in the world is fully justified in the eyes of God, *even though we haven't yet attained to our goal of full character development*, because the reality of our faith proclaims that we fully *intend* to attain this larger goal, no matter what may actually happen to us. Hence, as far as God is concerned, the reality of our present-day faith makes the eventual attainment of our developmental goal a virtual certainty, since it is only a matter of time until our faith makes this psychospiritual endpoint a reality.

This relationship between faith and salvation can be better illustrated by means of an analogy. Let's say that a grossly overweight college student approaches his school coach looking for a position on the track team. Judging from his present condition, it is clear that he cannot be allowed to join the team, because he is so terribly out of shape. But let's say that he is also very strongly motivated to be the fastest runner in the entire city; so much so, in fact, that he promises the coach that he will quickly lose 100 pounds and get into tip-top shape if he is given a provisional acceptance onto the team. Now, it is evident that if the student's motivation to succeed is sufficiently intense, the coach can justifiably offer him a provisional place on the team, because the student's inner motivational state more or less guarantees that he will rapidly live up to his word and become an outstanding athlete.

Moving on with our analogy, let's say that the coach does indeed offer the student a provisional acceptance onto the team, and that six months later the student does in fact become the fastest teenager in the state. At this point, the coach's decision to offer him a provisional place on the team will have clearly paid off—and thereby have completely justified itself—because of the student's tremendous success at losing weight and getting into shape.

It is clear that the student's enormous success in this example was directly related to his own faith in himself, because it is our degree of faith in our own abilities that determines how strongly motivated we are to achieve any given goal. We see, then, that based upon the student's tremendous faith in himself, the coach's initial decision to accept him onto the team was fully justified, not by the student's initial athletic capacity as an obese individual, *but rather by his future promise to excel, based upon his present-day amount of faith.* In this sense, the student actually saved himself as far as his own future membership on the track team was concerned, because he was able to transform his faith into constructive action.

Interestingly enough, our provisional faith-based acceptance into the kingdom of heaven is much the same way, insofar as our initial salvation by faith is fully justified in the eyes of God by our future promise to grow to our own full development. It is clear, though, that only the highest level of faith will function in this capacity, because nothing less will typically suffice to guarantee our own future sanctification. *Put another way, God will only agree to save us by faith when our faith is sufficiently intense to make our future sanctification a virtual certainty.*

Sanctification is thus our ultimate psychospiritual goal in this world. To be sanctified, of course, means to be fully individuated or developed, and this is something that we ourselves are ultimately responsible for. Faith is simply the inner motivational power that propels us in the right direction. We are therefore saved by faith, not because faith is sufficient in and of itself in the eyes of God to save us, but because faith is the inner orienting power that directs us to the true goal of our lives: our own eventual sanctification, or full character development.

James' epistle agrees with this contention:

What good is it, my brothers, if a man claims to have faith but has no deeds? Can such faith save him?

Suppose a brother or sister is without clothes and daily food. If one says to him, "Go, I wish you well; keep warm and well fed," but does nothing about his physical needs, what good is it? In the same way, faith by itself, if it is not accompanied by action, is dead.

But someone will say, "You have faith; I have deeds."

Show me your faith without deeds, and I will show you my faith by what I do. You believe that there is one God. Good! [But] even the demons believe that—and shudder.

You foolish man, do you want evidence that faith without deeds is useless? Was not our ancestor Abraham considered righteous for what he did when he offered his son Isaac on the altar? You see that his faith and his actions were working together, and his faith was made complete by what he did. And the scripture was fulfilled that says, "Abraham believed God, and it was credited to him as righteousness," and he was called God's friend. You see that a person is justified by what he does and not by faith alone . . . As the body without the spirit is dead, so faith without deeds is dead (James 2:14–26).

It is this proclamation that makes the definition of a true Christian very sobering. For as far as most people are concerned, all it takes to be a genuine Christian is a personal affirmation of the Lordship of Jesus Christ. But is this truly all that is necessary? Apparently not, for as James deftly points out, even the demons themselves believe, and tremble! Clearly something more is required before one can be considered to be an authentic Christian, and according to James, this extra something is simply the personal willingness to *act on* one's inner belief (James 2:26). This assertion is perfectly consistent with our claim that self-actualization is the ultimate goal of human life, because we can only become fully individuated when we act upon our inner faith and do what is necessary to maximize our own internal development.

It follows from this observation that the single most important thing about being a Christian is following Christ's Example in one's own life. For if we really and truly believe in Jesus, we will *automatically* go about trying to emulate Him in every relevant way we can, even to the point of going to the cross in our own lives and crucifying the evil and neurotic parts of our innermost selves. Anything less is totally inadequate, as Jesus Himself confirms in the following passage from the Gospel of Matthew:

> "Not everyone who says to me, 'Lord, Lord' will enter the kingdom of heaven, but only he who does the will of my Father who is in heaven. Many will say to me on that day, 'Lord, Lord, did we not prophecy in your name, and in your name drive out demons and perform many miracles?' Then I will tell them plainly, 'I never knew you. Away from me, you evildoers!'
>
> Therefore everyone who hears these words of mine *and puts them into practice* is like a wise man who built his house on the rock. The rain came down, the streams rose, and the winds blew and beat against that house; yet it did not fall, because it had its foundation on the rock. But everyone who hears these words of mine and does not put them into practice is like a foolish man who built his house on sand. The rain came down, the streams rose, and the winds blew and beat against that house, and it fell with a great crash" (Matt. 7:21–27, emphasis mine).

There is a very good reason why we will only be acceptable to God when we put His words into action: because it is only by acting on the developmental principles that were set forth in Christ's life that we can succeed in bringing our characters to a relative state of completion, and only fully completed personalities are intrinsically worthy enough to enter the kingdom of heaven.

Acting on God's word is thus like the wise man who built his house on the rock. The rock, of course, represents the stable foundation of a healthy, well-built personality, which is able to withstand the many storms of life because it is not weakened by any significant degree of character pathology.

Moreover, this type of fully developed individual has more or less transcended her tendency to do evil because she is mature enough to *want* to do the good, and she is wise enough to know precisely *how* to go about doing it.

It is thus the psychospiritual goal of individuation, or full character development, that is the "do-all, end-all" for traditional Christian theology. It is the chief purpose for which we were created (at least at this early stage in our development), and it is the ultimate criterion that will be used to determine who is worthy enough to enter the kingdom of heaven, and who isn't.

Interestingly enough, the Bible agrees wholeheartedly with this fundamental message. For in Matthew's Gospel Jesus tells us to be "perfect," even as our Father in heaven is perfect (Matt. 5:48). As John Sanford has pointed out, this is one of the most misunderstood verses in the entire Bible.[34] For the Greek word that is translated as "perfect" here—*teleios*—literally means "brought to completion," or "brought to an appropriate end state." In other words, Jesus is admonishing us to become fully developed, because this is the only way that we will ever be found to be worthy enough to enter the kingdom of heaven.

This is welcome relief for millions of people who thought that they had to conform to a strict one-sided view of perfection in order to be acceptable to God. Fortunately for all of us, nothing could be further from the truth, because God knows that we are simply incapable of absolute character perfection at the present time. As a consequence, He doesn't expect anything of the sort from us. But what He *does* expect is that we do our very best to actualize ourselves, even if it means breaking a few rules here and there in the process.

It is, to the contrary, the Satanic side of our innermost conscience that wants us to believe that we have to be absolutely perfect in the here-and-now in order to be acceptable to God. This is the sort of inaccurate belief that is able to sabotage our present-day lives very effectively, because it simply isn't possible for any of us to attain to this lofty goal as of yet, so those who nevertheless feel compelled to attain it are liable to fall prey to despair and to give up their faith and hope in God in the process. This in turn tends to strongly inhibit their inner progress towards full character development.

Ideally speaking, we should strive for moral and developmental excellence as much as we possibly can, while simultaneously recognizing that we are still grossly imperfect at the present time. This sort of realization will go a long way towards facilitating our psychospiritual development, because it tells us in no uncertain terms that we have a long way to go until we become fully individuated. At the same time, we should do our very best to forgive both ourselves and others for the sins that we can't help committing, because this not only will help to make our world a better place in which to live, it will also help to alleviate our own inner sense of guilt as well.

Eliphaz's First Speech

After waiting a week to say something, Job's friend Eliphaz finally speaks up in Chapter Four. Reflecting the dominant belief at the time, Eliphaz tries to convince Job that his suffering is due to some unknown sin that he has committed:

"If someone ventures a word with you, will you be impatient? But who can keep from speaking?

Think how you have instructed many, how you have strengthened feeble hands. Your words have supported those who stumbled; you have strengthened faltering knees. But now trouble comes to you and you are discouraged; it strikes you, and you are dismayed. Should not your piety be your confidence and your blameless ways your hope?

Consider now: Who, being innocent, has ever perished? Where were the upright ever destroyed? As I have observed, those who plow evil and those who sow trouble reap it. At the breath of God they are destroyed; at the blast of his anger the perish.

. . . Can a mortal be more righteous than God? Can a man be more pure than his Maker? If God places no trust in His servants, if he charges his angels with error, how much more those who live in houses of clay, whose foundations are in the dust, who are crushed more readily than a moth!

. . . Call if you will, but who will answer you? To which of the holy ones will you turn? Resentment kills a fool, and envy slays the simple. I myself have seen a fool taking root, but suddenly his house was cursed. His children are far from safety, crushed in court without a defender. The hungry consume his harvest, taking it even from among thorns, and the thirsty pant after his wealth. For hardship does not spring from the soil, nor does trouble sprout from the ground. Yet man is born to trouble as surely as sparks fly upward.

. . . Blessed is the man whom God corrects; so do not despise the discipline of the Almighty. For he wounds, but he also binds up; he injures, but his hands also heal. From six calamities he will rescue you; in seven no harm will befall you. In famine he will ransom you from death, and in battle from the stroke of the sword. You will be protected from the lash of the tongue, and need not fear when destruction comes. You will laugh at destruction and famine, and need not fear the beasts of the earth. For you will have a covenant with the stones of the field, and the wild animals will be at peace with you. You will know that your tent is secure; you will take stock of your property and find nothing missing. You will know that your children will be many, and your descendants like the grass of the earth. You will come to the grave in full vigor, like sheaves gathered in season" (Job 4:2–9,17–19; 5:1–7,17–26).

In one sense Eliphaz is very much correct in what he tells Job. He is correct in his assertion that Job's suffering is somehow related to his sinful condition as a human being. For as we have seen before, *all* suffering is related in one way or another to our sinful existence as partially developed free agents, because we can't help but be sinful—and therefore prone to pain and suffering—in our present state of character immaturity. This is why the Bible can tell us that *all* have sinned and therefore come short of the glory of God (Rom. 3:23): because we *all* presently exist in a sinful state of partial character assembly, and this automatically includes Job. While Job may have been a better person overall than most of the other people of his time, it does *not* follow from this statement that he was truly sinless or perfect.

Indeed, the Bible tells us that the only sinless person who ever lived was Jesus, so by the Bible's own account Job could *not* have been sinless. But even Jesus had to suffer in order to attain His God-given purpose on earth, so there is no reason to believe that Job should have suffered any less. If anything, Job's suffering, horrible though it may have been, did not even approach Jesus' inconceivable level of anguish on the cross, so Job's pain wasn't theologically out of place as far as the teaching of the Bible is concerned.

In fact, if moral evil (or sin) can ultimately be traced back to a lack of full character development in the human personality (which it clearly can), then it is our own partial character assembly that is *itself* sinful, at least insofar as it is regularly responsible for producing most forms of behavioral destructiveness in the world.[35]

In this sense, and in this sense only, can we say that Job's suffering was "caused" by his personal "sinfulness." But this isn't to say that Job had done anything wrong *per se* in his day-to-day life to deserve his torment; it is simply to say that as a fallible creature of God who was living in the necessary human condition of intrinsic sinfulness, Job couldn't help but find himself in a world and body which are themselves slanted towards the generation of pain and suffering. The unsavory consequence of this existential situation is that no matter how good he was in his worldly life, he was nevertheless subject to horrible diseases and catastrophic physical calamities, all as a function of his mere existence as a human being.

Therefore, Eliphaz was blatantly wrong when he tried to connect Job's suffering to any *specific* wrong that Job might have committed in his life. For it simply isn't the case that Job could have prevented most (or all) of his personal calamities by behaving in a different fashion. These kinds of evils can happen to anyone, regardless of how good or bad they happen to be in their lives.

On the other hand, it is still very much a possibility for us to bring evil upon ourselves in the here-and-now because of our sinful behavior. The arrested drug addict, for instance, who experiences a violent process of drug withdrawal in jail has obviously brought his problems upon himself. Job's calamities, however, were apparently not of this self-inflicted type. There was no way that he could have indirectly caused the violent storm that killed his children (although he could conceivably have built a stronger house for them to live in that might have been capable of surviving the storm). Similarly, there is no way that Job could have prevented the Sabeans and Chaldeans from stealing his oxen, camels, and donkeys (though once again, it is conceivable that he could have built a better fortress to protect his livestock from possible theft). And finally, there is no way that Job could have prevented the "fire of God" from raining out of the sky and killing his sheep.

In short, Job's calamities were primarily of a passive type, insofar as they weren't brought on by anything that Job himself had directly done; they were, rather, caused by the dangerous and unpredictable world that he had no choice but to live in. The upshot here is that we are *all* eminently prone to these kinds of destructive influences in our lives, not because of anything specific that we have done *per se*, but simply because we are human beings who *necessarily* must live in a dangerous world, at least at this early stage in our development.

Eliphaz was thus correct when he told Job that God will take care of him in the end. Blessed indeed is the man whom the Lord corrects, because he will end up growing to the point that he will eventually become worthy of the kingdom of God. For once this heavenly point is finally reached, the individual will indeed "laugh" at destruction and famine, because he will realize that these physical trials are no longer necessary to coax him into further levels of spiritual growth.

Job's Reply

Job's response to Eliphaz's stinging tirade is intense and heart-wrenching. He doesn't know why God has chosen to inflict harm on him; all he knows is that he has done his very best to be good in his life, but all to seemingly no avail.

> "If only my anguish could be weighed and all my misery be placed on the scales! It would surely outweigh the sand of the seas—no wonder my words have been impetuous. The arrows of the Almighty are in me, my spirit drinks in their poison; God's terrors are marshaled against me . . .

Oh, that I might have my request, that God would grant what I hope for, that God would be willing to crush me, to let loose his hand and cut me off! Then I would still have this consolation—my joy in unrelenting pain—that I had not denied the words of the Holy One" (Job 6: 1–4, 8–10).

Job's faith in the goodness and righteousness of God is truly incredible. Even though he has lost his wealth, health, and his family, he still feels motivated to be respectful to his Creator, and this in spite of the fact that he knows that he has done nothing wrong above and beyond his mere existence as a human being to deserve his torment.

This in turn raises a very important question: from whence does our suffering *ultimately* originate? Is it a direct punishment for sin that has been meted out from the depths of the spiritual world, or is it a natural consequence of what we do in our lives? In Biblical times the former explanation was generally believed; it was simply assumed that people were directly rewarded or punished for their behavior by beings who resided in the spiritual realm. This is why Job's friends accuse him of some sort of sinful wrongdoing: because they can't imagine that his suffering is unrelated to any specific behaviors on his part.

It is also for this reason that Bildad the Shuhite's view of Job's transgression is more accurate and realistic than that which was promulgated by his other two friends. Bildad doesn't attempt to locate the source of Job's wrongdoing in any *specific* wrongs that Job might have committed; he instead locates it in Job's very *humanity*, as the following passage well illustrates:

"Dominion and awe belong to God; he establishes order in the heights of heaven. Can his forces be numbered? Upon whom does his light not rise? How then can a man be righteous before God? How can one born of woman be pure? If even the moon is not bright and the stars are not pure in his eyes, how much less man, who is but a maggot—a son of man, who is only a worm" (Job 25:2–6)?

This is actually a very Christian point of view, for the Bible repeatedly tells us that "there is no one righteous, not even one" (Rom. 3:10). But if this is true, then it must also have been true of Job, because no matter how good Job may have been in relation to his fellow citizens, he was still human, so he was still plagued with the same sorts of problems that afflict *all* people. Indeed, Jesus is said to have been the only human being who ever lived who failed to sin, yet He suffered the worst death imaginable on the cross as the ultimate example for all of us to follow. Now, if the only perfect human being who ever lived had to suffer in order to rise to a higher life, then how much *more* necessary must it be for the rest of us—including Job—to suffer horrifically as well?

Job, however, finds it difficult to understand that his suffering isn't directly related to any specific wrongdoing that he has committed. Instead, he stubbornly tries to maintain his innocence to his friends:

> "As surely as God lives, who has denied me justice, the Almighty, who has made me taste bitterness of soul, as long as I have life within me, the breath of God in my nostrils, my lips will not speak wickedness, and my tongue will utter no deceit . . . till I die, I will not deny my integrity. I will maintain my righteousness and never let go of it; my conscience will not reproach me as long as I live" (Job 27: 2–6).

It is precisely here that Job's true guilt begins to manifest itself. For by stubbornly proclaiming his absolute innocence in the eyes of God, he ends up committing one of the greatest sin of them all: hubris. No honest human being can proclaim his across-the-board innocence before God because we are *all* sinful, and therefore in need of our just due in life. Like the Pharisees who came after him, Job has apparently been fooled by his own upright behavior into believing that he is beyond Divine reproach, but this is clearly nothing more than egregious self-deception. No one but Jesus (for the Christian) is beyond Divine reproach, but even He suffered immensely in order to teach us a lesson. There is therefore no reason whatsoever for believing that Job was completely innocent and blameless before God.

Job asserts that God has denied him justice on account of his exorbitant suffering, but it must be remembered that nowhere in the Bible are we ever promised that our day-to-day experiences in this world will directly mirror what we deserve, or think we deserve, from God. This is the Hindu law of karma, and while it may be true to a certain extent, it clearly isn't true all the time, because there are many events that take place in our lives that we *don't* directly elicit or otherwise deserve. Indeed, the only time we can expect such a close alignment between what we deserve in our lives and what we actually receive is in the Afterlife, but this point has obviously not been reached yet.

There is, however, one place where we *do* in fact get what we deserve in this life: our own inner spirit or personality. For insofar as our innermost self directly responds in either a positive or negative growth-related fashion to each thing we do in this world, then we *do* actually get what we deserve on the inside, because this change is internalized in our personality forevermore. However, our inner just due is often not reflected in the outer events of our lives, which is why we can say that we don't always get what we deserve in this lifetime. The Law of Karma can thus be seen to apply without exception to the *inner* life of the soul, but since there is typically a significant disproportion between our inner and outer realities, the Law of Karma can't always be credited for causing each and every event that happens to us in this world. For the most part, however, the Law of Karma *will* end up causing a progressively larger proportion of those events that will happen to us in the future, because of the fact that *we* tend to frame, through our own internally-driven behaviors, the circumstances that we will have to contend with in the future.

Job, however, doesn't seem to be aware of the fact that there isn't always a one-to-one correspondence between a person's daily experiences and his or her behavior in this world. To the contrary, he naively expects his daily experiences to directly mirror his outer goodness in all instances, so it is no surprise that he believes that God has done him a tremendous injustice.

Indeed, Job is clearly convinced that he can maintain his righteousness by not directly blaspheming the name of God. But what he doesn't seem to realize is that this very belief is *itself* wicked, because "all our righteous acts are like filthy rags" in the eyes of God (Isa. 64:6), *especially* self-righteousness. Job is thus guilty of inadvertently confusing his outer behavior for inner truth, but unfortunately for him, God doesn't regard our outer behavior only. Rather, He looks inward at the heart and, as a consequence of this, He recognizes that no matter what we may happen to do in our lives, we can't *possibly* be fully righteous at this point in our development.

Interestingly enough, though, Job turns out to be far more stoic in his suffering than his wife, who urges him to "curse God and die" soon after his evils befall him (Job 2:9). She does this because she thinks it is ridiculous for him to try to maintain his righteousness in spite of his horrendous condition. Job, however, correctly responds to her by asserting that we cannot accept good from God without accepting trouble also. This is certainly true enough, so the Bible concludes that "in all this, Job did not sin in what he said" (Job 2:10).

The key here is that Job's sin wasn't so much in what he said as it was in the inner state of his heart. For while he may not have openly cursed God with his lips, he was nevertheless full of hubris deep inside, not to mention the inner developmental evil that we are *all* infected with at this stage in our lives.

God's Response to Job

Once Job and his friends get a chance to repeatedly express their innermost feelings, God finally answers Job out of the whirlwind, in one of the most famous speeches to be found anywhere:

> "Who is this that darkens my counsel with words without knowledge? Brace yourself like a man; I will question you, and you shall answer me. Where were you when I laid the earth's foundation? Tell me if you understand. Who marked off its dimensions? Surely you know! Who stretched a mea-

suring line across it? On what were its footings set, or who laid its cornerstone—while the morning stars sang together and all the angels shouted for joy?

Who shut up the sea behind doors when it burst forth from the womb, when I made the clouds its garment and wrapped it in thick darkness, when I fixed limits for it and set its doors and bars in place, when I said, 'This far you may come and no farther; here is where your proud waves halt'?" (Job 38:2-11).

When the first part of God's magnificent speech is over, Job has the courage to briefly utter the following response:

"I am unworthy—how can I reply to you? I put my hand over my mouth. I spoke once, but I have no answer—twice, but I will say no more" (Job 40:4-5).

In spite of this protestation of unworthiness, Job still hasn't heard enough from God to motivate him to repent from his proud ways. So, God continues to humble him in relentless fashion:

"Brace yourself like a man; I will question you, and you shall answer me.

Would you discredit my justice? Would you condemn me to justify yourself? Do you have an arm like God's, and can your voice thunder like his? Then adorn yourself with glory and splendor, and clothe yourself in honor and majesty. Unleash the fury of your wrath, look at every proud man and bring him low, look at every proud man and humble him, crush the wicked where they stand. Bury them all in the dust together; shroud their faces in the grave. Then I myself will admit to you that your own right hand can save you. . . .

Can you pull in the leviathan with a fishhook or tie down his tongue with a rope? Can you put a cord through his nose or pierce his jaw with a hook? Will he keep begging you for mercy? Will he speak to you with gentle words? Will he make an agreement with you for you to take him as your slave for life?

Can you make a pet of him like a bird or put him on a leash for your girls? Will traders barter for him? Will they divide him up among the merchants? Can you fill his hide with harpoons or his head with fishing spears? If you lay a hand on him, you will remember the struggle and never do it again! Any hope of subduing him is false; the mere sight of him is overpowering. No one is fierce enough to rouse him. . . . Nothing on earth is his equal— a creature without fear. He looks down on all that are haughty; he is king over all that are proud" (Job 40:7-14; 41:1-10, 33-34).

In this passage God directly tells us that it is *pride* that is separating Job from true righteousness. This is why He goes to the trouble of showing Job how weak and impotent he really is—so he can be shown how inappropriate it really is for a fallible human being to feel proud and unrepentant.

Finally, after being humiliated by God into complete submission, Job gives in and repents:

> "I know that you can do all things; no plan of yours can be thwarted. You asked, 'Who is this that obscures my counsel without knowledge?' Surely I spoke of things I did not understand, things too wonderful for me to know.
>
> You said, 'Listen now, and I will speak; I will question you, and you shall answer me.' My ears had heard of you but now my eyes have seen you. Therefore I despise myself and repent in dust and ashes" (Job 42:2–6).

In the above quotation the implication is made that Job had to "see God" before he could truly repent in "dust and ashes." If we can generalize this necessity over to all people, we find that we *all* must somehow see God before we can repent in a theologically acceptable fashion. This can be understood to mean that we must repeatedly suffer in our lives if we truly want to repent, because this is the only way that our pride can be whittled down to nothing.

The word "repent," as we have seen, comes from the Greek word *metanoia*, which means "to turn around 180 degrees." Thus, to repent means to do a complete about-face in one's life, and this is understandably a very difficult task for most people to accomplish. This is why we must often "hit bottom" before we can truly repent and change for the better: because most people will only agree to change when they are left with no other option in their lives.

God's magnificent tirade is thus designed to teach Job one important lesson: that we are supposed to trust in the ultimate power and goodness of God *no matter what happens to us*. This is the point that God is trying to make as He repeatedly humbles Job into submission with His incomparable scientific insight and supreme Creative Power. Since God is all there is, and since He is in total control of all things, it is thoroughly rational for us to trust Him no matter how much we may happen to suffer in our lives.

This lesson is exceedingly important, because we all suffer from unfair evils from time to time. Indeed, millions of people throughout the world suffer horrendously every single day, and many of them have done little or nothing to deserve such punishment. God's message to these individuals, spoken through the book of Job, is direct and to the point: no one should let their suffering cause them to give up hope in the transcendent goodness of life, because the Supreme God of the universe is ultimately in control, and He is going to be able to transform these evils into genuine goods in the end.

Indeed, John Hick believes that our future glory in heaven is going to be so substantive that it is going to end up justifying *all* the evils that have occurred on the way to it. This is a very positive message that fits in well with God's message in the book of Job. Everything is indeed going to work out in the end, no matter how bad we may happen to be suffering at the present time. This is exceedingly good news, because it gives us the hope and encouragement that we so desperately need in order to continue living in such a difficult, pain-filled world.

The book of Job finally draws to a close with Job regaining all that he had possessed before, and then some:

> After Job had prayed for his friends, the Lord made him prosperous again and gave him twice as much as he had before. All his brothers and sisters and everyone who had known him before came and ate with him in his house. They comforted and consoled him over all the trouble the Lord had brought upon him, and each one gave him a piece of silver and a gold ring.
>
> The Lord blessed the latter part of Job's life more than the first. He had fourteen thousand sheep, six thousand camels, a thousand yoke of oxen and a thousand donkeys. And he also had seven sons and three daughters. . . . Nowhere in all the land were there found women as beautiful as Job's daughters, and their father granted them an inheritance along with their brothers. After this, Job lived a hundred and forty years; he saw his children and their children to the fourth generation. And so he died, old and full of years (Job 42:10–13, 15–17).

The fact that God blessed the second part of Job's life more than the first can be taken to mean that sin, followed by suffering and redemption, is inherently more valuable than blind innocence for its own sake. This is why it was better, all things considered, for Adam to sin and to suffer than it would have been for him to have remained in the Garden of Eden forever. This is the "O felix culpa" (O fortunate crime) theme that was such a big part of the early Church, and it is plainly evident here, because true individuation is only possible in a world in which sin is followed by suffering, repentance and redemption. This is the basic Christian message writ large, and it applies just as much to us today as it did to Adam and Eve or Job. Best of all, it promises to bring lasting happiness to everyone in the eschaton, because it will miraculously transform all the evils that have ever occurred on this planet into the greatest of goods.

Contingency, Necessity, and the Ultimate Transformation of Evil into Good

Many have criticized as incoherent this idea that there will be a future good so great that it will end up justifying all the evils that led up to it. After all, it is hard to see how such horrendous evils as Hiroshima and Dachau could ever be justified by *any* type of future good, no matter how great. This was Ivan's basic idea in Fyodor Dostoevsky's *The Brothers Karamazov*; namely, that no future good based on the suffering of even a single innocent child is worth the "price of admission." And certainly, if we confine our attention only to the world of contingent events, it is very difficult to see how any given evil could possibly be justified at all by a future good, because there is a very definite sense in which contingent events might not have ever happened, in which case our world, including the world of the future, would have been a better place overall.

Everything changes, however, if we shift our focus from the realm of the contingent to the realm of the metaphysically necessary, for if it is the case that all contingent evils are the result of a deeper metaphysical necessity[36] that is required for our own existence, then these contingent evils could indeed plausibly be justified by a deeper level of structural necessity, but *only* if these underlying necessities eventually lead to a future good that will be so great that it will somehow end up being worth the "price of admission."

Interestingly enough, the underlying structural conditions that are necessary to support human existence do indeed seem to entail a certain amount of necessary evil, due once again to the unique confluence of humankind's essential properties, which seem to entail a temporary amount of evil by their very nature. To the extent that this is so, this would mean that *no* form of human existence would be possible in the absence of a certain amount of contingent evil. This would render it necessary for these contingent evils to be *possible*, which in turn would make them *indirectly* necessary when they occur, even though their individual occurrences would themselves remain contingent. *It is this indirect necessity that transforms contingent evils into indirectly necessary ones, and this, in turn, makes it possible that all contingent evils will themselves be justified in the eschaton by a future good that will be so great that it will automatically end up justifying all the evils that led up to it.*

Notes

1. It is interesting to note that this process of regulating who gets into the kingdom and who doesn't is probably not one that is mediated by an external being. Rather, this process of spiritual selection appears to be something that will happen naturally inside of our own souls whenever the time is right (i.e., whenever we begin to approximate our own full development). We mustn't forget Jesus' dictum that the kingdom of heaven is within us (Luke 17:21). For insofar as this is indeed the case, it follows that *we* are the only ones who are preventing our free forward movement into the kingdom, through our own pervasive lack of inner maturity.
2. This view of God is highly problematic for the traditional theologian, because it enthrones evil forever by making it part of God's eternal nature. This is very

much at odds with the traditional view of the Godhead, which sees God as an entirely benevolent Being.
3. The reason for this relative sameness over time is that God has to remain partly evil *forever* in order to fulfill this particular definition of wholeness; and this, in turn, makes any instrumental view of evil impossible by definition, because instrumental forms of evil self-dissipate when their underlying goal is achieved.
4. David Ray Griffin, *God, Power, and Evil* (Philadelphia: The Westminster Press, 1976), pp. 21–23.
5. For a more thorough explanation of this relationship between evil and the Human Essence, please refer to my forthcoming book *Evil and the Essence of Humanity*.
6. I am adopting J.L. Mackie's concept of second-order omnipotence here, in which God freely chose to limit His own power over His human creatures by giving them genuine free will. This voluntary self-limitation on the part of God thus denies the absolute omnipotence of God in the *present* universe, but simultaneously preserves God's ultimate control over His own state of relative power, since it assumes that He *originally* had all the power that it is possible for one being to have prior to His voluntary decision to create self-determining human beings *ex nihilo*. The advantage of this theoretical maneuver is that it is able to preserve the overall concept of omnipotence in spite of all the free will-inspired human evil in the world. It is also able to preserve the doctrine of omnipotence in the face of genuine human freedom over against God.
7. This is a doctrine of Divine necessity that lies beyond the scope of this book, but the reader is directed to Alvin Plantinga's outstanding work *The Nature of Necessity* for a complete treatment of this provocative issue.
8. Erich Fromm, *The Anatomy of Human Destructiveness* (New York: Holt, Rinehart, and Winston, 1973), pp. 268–433.
9. This phenomenon of escalating evil doesn't accumulate continuously in a linear fashion over the years, however, because each successive generation starts anew in the human life cycle, albeit in tune with the socialization policies of the preceding generation. This introduction of "new blood" into each successive generation enables both the positive and negative socialization policies of the society to regularly be overhauled throughout the historical process. Unfortunately, this doesn't always ensure that negative policies will be eliminated before they cause harm to large numbers of people, because of the extreme mind-seducing power that is inherent in *any* society.
10. Many anti-theodicists have questioned the necessity of a world that is characterized by fixed natural laws, because these laws are indirectly responsible for causing much human suffering. As Bruce Reichenbach has pointed out, however, fixed laws are necessary if we are to have free will, because freedom presupposes the existence of a predictable causal system, which clearly would not exist had our world not been governed by fixed natural laws.
11. Blaise Pascal, *Pensées*, quoted in Rollo May's *Psychology and the Human Dilemma* (New York: W.W. Norton & Co., 1967), p. 25.
12. In the first part of Job 28:28 we're told that wisdom is the fear of the Lord, but this doesn't mean that we literally need to be afraid of our Creator. Rather, the original Hebrew word that is translated as "fear" here, *yir'ah,* can also refer to a pious sense of respect and reverence for God. Thus, a more meaningful translation of this phrase might be, "Respect and reverence for God—that is wisdom." This makes good sense as far as the intrinsic accuracy of our thoughts are concerned, because the only way we can be objectively correct in many of our religously-oriented assumptions about the world is if we are first correct about

the possible existence of God. Thus, if God actually exists, the only person who will end up being objectively correct about this sort of religiously-oriented knowledge is the one who has first properly acknowledged the existence of a larger Creator.

13. St. Paul's use of the concept of adoption in his letters to the Romans and Galatians is particularly revealing, because it shows us the extent to which our lives are truly our own, and not God's. This is due to the fact that we have been given near complete control over our lives through the vehicle of free will; so much so, in fact, that God *cannot* coerce us to do anything against our will without violating our essential freedom. This self-limitation on the part of God effectively removes Him from direct ownership over our lives, which explains St. Paul's use of the word "adopt" in Romans 8:15, 8:24, 9:4, and Galatians 4:5. Indeed, since we have been given more or less complete control over our own development, God has in effect bequeathed direct fathership over our own lives to us, which explains why He has to "adopt" us back into His spiritual family when we reach a certain level of psychospiritual maturity.

14. Interestingly enough, the Greek word that is translated as "perfect" in Matthew 5:48 is *teleios*, which literally means "brought to an appropriate end state." Hence, the very essence of Biblical perfection is developmental in nature.

15. I am assuming here a state of *relative* character assembly. For while we may never cease growing throughout the rest of eternity, there is a very real sense in which we will eventually become optimally individuated. It is at this point that we will have reached full character assembly, even though we will continue learning and growing forevermore.

16. John A. Sanford, *Evil: The Shadow Side of Reality*, p. 40.

17. Even if this hypothetical transformation of evil into good actually transpires one day, it will only hold true because the underlying structural parameters of the world temporarily necessitated the existence of this type of instrumental evil. Contingent evil events, on the other hand, would *still* be evil when viewed in isolation; they would only be transformed into good when they are seen to be the contingent result of the underlying structural parameters of our world, which are themselves necessary.

18. Richard Swinburne, "Natural Evil," in *The Problem of Evil*, Michael L. Peterson, ed. (Notre Dame: University of Notre Dame Press, 1992), pp. 303–315; and Bruce Reichenbach, *Evil and a Good God* (New York: Fordham University Press, 1982), pp. 87–118.

19. Please see my forthcoming *Evil and the Essence of Humanity* for more on this intriguing subject.

20. This "sharpness" appears to be directly proportional to an evil event's perceived degree of averseness.

21. Interestingly enough, the word "excruciating" has a Christian-related origin, insofar as it literally means "out of a cross." Hence the word excruciating literally refers to the inconceivable amount of pain that is generated by the process of crucifixion.

22. John A. Sanford, *The Kingdom Within*, pp. 49, 51–52.

23. Charles Caldwell Ryrie, *The Ryrie Study Bible, New International Version* (Chicago: Moody Press, 1986), p. 678.

24. Ernest Becker, *The Denial of Death*, pp. 47–67.

25. Surely it cannot be a coincidence that the Biblical description of hell matches so precisely our modern understanding of depth psychology, as well as the time-honored description of hell given in *The Tibetan Book of the Dead*. Theoretical

convergences such as these generally only happen when great human truths are involved, because these timeless ideas typically reveal themselves in a number of different ways to a wide variety of people.
26. John Hick, *Death and Eternal Life* (San Francisco: Harper & Row, 1976), pp. 414–415.
27. Guru Rinpoche, *The Tibetan Book of the Dead*, transl. by Francesca Fremantle and Chögyam Trungpa (Boston: Shambhala, 1987), pp. 75–77.
28. John A. Sanford, *The Kingdom Within*, pp. 86–87.
29. John Hick, *Death and Eternal Life*, pp. 250–261.
30. John Hick, *Evil and the God of Love*, p. 342.
31. John Hick, *Death and Eternal Life*, p. 201.
32. John Hick, *Evil and the God of Love*, p. 344.
33. This is the sense in which Kant believed that well-intentioned behaviors were moral, even if they had destructive consequences in the world. Since morality is inextricably tied to the process of character development, and since our characters are directly affected by our inner intentions, and not solely by the outer consequences of our behavior, it follows that our behavior can indeed be moral even if the outer consequences of that behavior are inadvertently destructive.
34. John A. Sanford, *Evil: The Shadow Side of Reality* (New York: Crossroad, 1981), p. 80.
35. From a larger God's-eye view, however, our temporary existence as partially-assembled individuals doesn't appear to be genuinely sinful at all, because it is presumably the only way there is for us to reach the final glorious endpoint that we are all naturally striving for on this planet.
36. My use of the word "metaphysical" in this context differs significantly from that of the process theist, who uses the concept of metaphysical necessity to refer to those unchangable aspects of the universe that would have obtained in *any* possible world. My usage of the word, by contrast, is much more limited, since I am using it to apply to those features of the world that are necessary *once the Human Essence has been instantiated*. Thus, had God instantiated a world devoid of human beings, my concept of metaphysical necessity would no longer be applicable.

CHAPTER FOUR
Evil in the Old Testament

Evil, Monotheism, and the Divine Goodness

The view of evil that is found in the Old Testament is decidedly different from that found in the New Testament. The New Testament, for instance, contains numerous references to Satan as an external being, and it clearly blames him for inciting much of the evil that takes place in our world. The Old Testament, on the other hand, contains only four limited references to Satan (Zech. 3:11; 1 Chron. 21:1; Psalm 109:6; and the various references contained in the book of Job). In each of these Old Testament sources, Satan is referred to as an accuser, who somehow finds a way to influence human beings in a negative, destructive manner.

According to John Sanford, the reason for this relative paucity of references to Satan in the Old Testament has to do with the unique monotheistic perspective that the ancient Hebrews had towards the reality of evil in the world.[1] For whereas the various New Testament writers chose to place most of the blame for evil on an external being named Satan, the Old Testament prophets had the courage to place the ultimate responsibility for evil squarely on the shoulders of God Himself. The chief advantage of this theoretical maneuver is that it preserves the absolute power of God throughout the universe.

This unflinching monotheism is central to both Judaism and Islam, but it seems to have been compromised to a certain extent in the New Testament, where Satan is repeatedly blamed for causing most of the evil in human affairs. Nevertheless, traditional Christian theology remains entirely monotheistic because God is believed to be ontologically superior to Satan in every relevant way. On this Christian view, God not only created Satan *ex nihilo*, He also tolerates Satan's continued existence, presumably because the latter is serving an important teleological function in the Divine Economy. This belief is supported by the symbolic interpretation of Satan as a personification of both moral and physical evil, because if Satan is merely the personification of evil only, and not an independent autonomous agency opposed to God, then he *cannot* be the immoral equivalent to God in any relevant capacity.

Monotheism is important because it is the only conceptualization of the Divine Power that holds up under rigorous logical analysis. For insofar as

God is truly omnipotent, there *cannot* be any other cosmic force sharing power with God *by definition*, because this would only serve to diminish God's all-power throughout the universe. Hence, the very doctrine of omnipotence demands an unqualified monotheism, and this, in turn, automatically renders any type of cosmic dualism necessarily false. C.S. Lewis describes the severe conceptual inadequacy of dualism in the following manner:

> The metaphysical difficulty is this. The two powers, the good and the evil, do not explain each other. Neither Ormuzd nor Ahriman can claim to be the Ultimate. More ultimate than either of them is the inexplicable fact of their being there together. Neither of them chose this tete-à-tete. Each of them, therefore, is *conditioned*—finds himself willy-nilly in a situation; and either that situation itself, or some unknown force which produced that situation, is the real Ultimate. Dualism has not yet reached the ground of being. You cannot accept two conditioned and mutually independent beings as the self-grounded, self-comprehending Absolute.[2]

We see, then, that the absolute monotheism of the Old Testament is refreshingly accurate from a strict theological perspective. However, it is the stark reality of evil in the world that seems to cast a shadow on this old-style theological monism, because the latter ultimately makes God responsible for all the evil events that have taken place on this planet. The book of Isaiah confirms this radical conclusion, as we have seen before:

> "I am the Lord, and there is none else . . . I form the light and create darkness: I make peace and create evil; I the Lord do all these things" (Isa. 45:5–7).

Amos 3:6 is equally direct in its description of God's metaphysical relationship to evil:

> Shall there be evil in a city, and the Lord hath not done it?

These verses make it clear that, for better or for worse, God is somehow ultimately responsible for all the evil events that have taken place in our world. On the face of it, this would seem to count against the perfect goodness of the Creator, but such a conclusion doesn't necessarily follow at all, as we have seen. For insofar as God has instantiated a Human Essence that is evil-prone by its very nature (at least temporarily), then He is only *indirectly* responsible for causing worldly evil, because He has merely created the underlying conditions by which moral and physical evil can occur. However, this doesn't necessarily implicate God as an immoral co-conspirator in the overall genesis of evil, because it is always possible that these underlying conditions are somehow necessary to the attainment of the greatest possible good for humanity.

The Stoic conceptualization of God as the Logos, or Logical Mediator between cause and effect, supports this monistic interpretation of God's relationship to evil, for while humans may be responsible for initiating the various efficient causes that bring about evil in the world, it is God as Logos who is responsible for bringing about the corresponding logical effects to these behaviors. In neither of these instances, however, can God be said to be *directly* responsible for generating evil events; He is, to the contrary, only *indirectly* responsible for them, via His initial creation of humanity and His metaphysical role as the Logical Mediator between cause and effect.

The science of quantum mechanics supports us in this monistic interpretation of the Godhead, since it has been conclusively demonstrated that our "concrete" physical world is actually comprised of a shadowy realm of subatomic particles that merely shows a statistical *tendency* to exist. Within this seemingly unpredictable quantum realm, in which legions of virtual particles are known to continually pop into and out of an invisible quantum field without apparent rhyme or reason, it is clear that some sort of larger synthetic force must be required to tie our macroscopic world of cause and effect together into a concrete physical whole; otherwise, the utter unpredictability that is characteristic of the subatomic realm would naturally carry through to our macroscopic world, and our lives would be a complete and total mess as a result (if indeed they would even be possible at all). This metaphysical synthetic force is a function that we can plausibly attribute to God, for if He is truly acting at the quantum level to tie humanly-inspired causes with their corresponding logical effects, then a concrete and stable world can indeed be generated by an underlying realm of "unpredictable" particles.

Interestingly enough, there is a passage in the book of Collosians that is remarkably consistent with this view of God as the ultimate principle of quantum coherence:

> For by him all things were created: things in heaven and on earth, visible *and invisible,* whether thrones or powers or rulers or authorities; all things were created by him and for him. He is before all things, *and in him all things hold together* (Col. 1:16–17, emphasis mine).

This view of God as Logos, however, can only be used to help explain God's relationship to *moral* evil, because human beings are the ones who are primarily responsible for generating this particular type of destructiveness. Physical evils, on the other hand, such as earthquakes, hurricanes, and the polio virus, are *not* directly attributable to the actions of human beings, since they have their origin in the underlying structure of the entire physical realm, which God Himself is said to have been directly responsible for. As a consequence, God can indeed be blamed in some sense for bringing about these physical evils (although human beings nevertheless tend to make themselves more susceptible than they have to be to physical evil through their own behavior).

But even here it is possible to take God off the hook, so to speak, since we can demonstrate that these natural evils are logically entailed by the necessary demands of the Human Essence.[3] To the extent that this is indeed the case, then God *cannot* be blamed for His creation of an evil-prone world, because in this instance He would only be bringing about those natural conditions that are truly essential for our own existence and continued development in this world.

In other words, given the apparent fact that God is 100 percent responsible for the character of the natural world we inhabit, either directly, through His creation of a destructive physical environment, or indirectly, through His creation of evil-prone human beings, the Old Testament actually portrays a more accurate image of the Godhead than the New Testament does, since it either directly or indirectly attributes everything that happens on this planet to God Himself. The New Testament, by contrast, places most of the blame for evil on Satan, probably because its writers felt uncomfortable attributing any type of worldly evil directly to God.

John Sanford has acknowledged the basic theological integrity displayed by the ancient Hebrew prophets in the following passage:

> It would be easy to dismiss the Old Testament image of God as primitive, something interesting perhaps from the point of view of the development of the idea of God, but not something we need take seriously any longer. Yet, for all of its primitive quality there is a basic integrity to the image of God that we find in pre-exilic biblical literature. We may be bothered by the idea that Yahweh sends good as well as evil, but it nevertheless presents us with a bold and unflinching monotheism. The ancient Hebrews, with their instinctive religious genius, were grasping the idea that there was one underlying reality to all phenomena, and if this meant that evil, as well as good, came from Yahweh, then this was a conclusion to be faced fearlessly.[4]

Once again, though, this radical monotheism shouldn't be understood to mean that God is responsible for directly initiating the world-based *efficient* causes that lead to evil. This *would* in fact be morally and theologically unacceptable, because it would then make the Creator directly culpable for each evil event that takes place in our world. There are two steps we can take, however, to maintain a morally acceptable version of Old Testament-style monotheism in the face of all the evil in our lives. First, we must attempt to put some degree of distance between God and evil by asserting that God is only responsible for generating the *underlying conditions* by which moral and natural evils can occur. But this clearly isn't enough in and of itself to get God off the hook, because in most instances it is just as morally wrong to set up the underlying conditions for evil as it is to commit the evil oneself. For instance, if I set up a situation whereby people feel uncontrollably compelled to physically abuse one another, then *I* am mostly responsible for the evil that they end up committing, even though they are the ones who actually do it, because I am the one who originally set up the underlying situation which promoted this sort of abusive behavior in the first place.

At first glance it is difficult to see why this principle of moral culpability for evil shouldn't also apply to God as well. After all, *He* is the One who is ultimately responsible for creating a natural order in which evil can occur, so it would seem that *He* should be the One who should receive the ultimate blame for our exceedingly destructive world. This appearance of culpability is bolstered by God's apparent refusal to intervene to prevent such unspeakably evil events as Auschwitz and Hiroshima from occurring.

It doesn't help to try to shift the blame to Adam, Eve, or the serpent either, because the fact remains that God is ultimately responsible for *their* evil-prone characters and behaviors just as much as He is for ours. It also doesn't help to try to blame the occurrence of evil on the unsearchable nature of human freedom, as St. Augustine tried to do, because genuine freedom of the will *doesn't* automatically translate into arbitrary choices that are made for no good reason at all. To the contrary, humans almost always make choices for a reason, and even when they don't, they nevertheless behave in strict accordance with their own internal nature; hence, they *still* could have been designed in such a way that they would have always *impulsively* made the right behavioral choices in their lives. Therefore, the mere fact that Adam and Eve went wrong in the Garden of Eden conclusively illustrates that they were originally created with some sort of serious *internal* impediment, which itself seems inconsistent with the existence of a perfectly good and all-powerful Deity. Once again we find that the mere existence of evil in the world seems to cast a dark and forbidding shadow on the nature of the Divine Being.

The only way out of this dilemma is to assert that our imperfect, evil-prone world is somehow *necessary* in a transcendent metaphysical sense before human existence can be possible. There are two possible ways in which this cosmic necessity can be interpreted. The first way is that which is espoused by the process theist, which posits a number of inviolable metaphysical principles that necessarily apply to *all* possible worlds. An example of this sort of metaphysical principle is the so-called necessary correlation[5] between value and power, due to David Griffin, which asserts that the more intrinsic value an entity possesses, the more potential power it will have for either good or evil.[6] This "solution" to the problem of evil succeeds only at the expense of the Divine Power, since the process theist believes that these necessary metaphysical principles must inevitably apply to *all* possible worlds, regardless of which particular objects God has chosen to instantiate in them.

The second way in which we can interpret the (possible) necessary nature of our world is in terms of the necessary nature of its principal inhabitant: humanity. For if it is indeed the case that humans have their own necessary nature, and if it is also the case that the Human Essence is the only one that God found to be worthwhile enough in itself to create a world for, then it follows that the intrinsic necessities that are specified by this essence will naturally provide the metaphysical boundary conditions for our world, and perhaps even for the universe as well.

This is clearly a level of necessity that flows, not out of the necessary nature of generic reality itself, but rather out of the necessary nature of a *particular essence*, which in this case is that possessed by human beings. The beauty of this theoretical perspective is that it preserves the omnipotence and perfect goodness of the Divine Power in the face of worldly evil, since it asserts that a temporary amount of evil is an intrinsically necessary (and therefore inevitable) feature of the Human Essence itself. According to this view, then, if genuine humans are going to be able to exist in the world, a certain amount of temporary evil is a *metaphysical necessity*. This essentialistic approach preserves the omnipotence of God because the instantiation of human beings without evil would in this case amount to a logical impossibility, and the Divine Power isn't generally held to be limited by such inherently contradictory tasks. The goodness of God is also preserved in this scenario as well, because God has, on this view, instantiated the best finite essence possible, *in spite of* its temporary proclivity to evil. God's absolute goodness is thus preserved by the presumption that the temporary fact of evil is *itself* necessary in an underlying structural sense if the greatest possible good, in this case represented by human beings, is to have a legitimate chance to exist and to prosper.

Of course, this begs the deeper question of why God had to have instantiated such an evil-prone essence to begin with, when He presumably could have instantiated one that is evil-free by its very nature. The only possible answer to this question is that God didn't find any other essence to be intrinsically desirable enough to be worth creating, all things considered. This answer isn't as untenable as it may initially seem, especially when our more desirable qualities as human beings are duly taken into consideration, such as our rationality, free will, and our independent and self-owned character structure. This position becomes even more persuasive if one holds that we were literally created in the Divine Spiritual Image, since only one finite representation of the Divine Being would seem to be possible, given the fixed metaphysical nature of God's underlying Essence.

What we are really arguing for in this case is that a certain amount of temporary evil is inherent in the very process of trying to mirror God's infinite spiritual qualities in finite form. Indeed, for all we know, such a task may actually be *infinitely* difficult, which could conceivably explain why our developmental task on this planet seems so arduous.

This position is also capable of explaining why God didn't just create us in a totally mature state to begin with. The answer to this question seems to be that it is metaphysically impossible for finite replicas of the Divine Spiritual Essence to be created instantaneously. Such a being must instead be created in an immature developmental state in order to make room for the essential quality of human freedom, which necessarily includes a number of other essential capacities as well, including the freedom to think, behave, and grow entirely as one pleases, with no significant type of coercion from without. In order for this to be possible, though, we must necessarily have as much control as possible over our own epistemological status in life, as well as over our degree of allegiance to our Maker. An instantaneously-created human saint, by contrast, wouldn't have access to *any* of these priceless qualities, since he or she would necessarily be preprogrammed to think and act in a certain predetermined way. This type of preprogramming is, of course, much more consistent with unfree automatons than it is with genuinely uncoerced humans, especially given the fact that the external infusion of *any* type of self-attainable knowledge into a being necessarily renders it more pre-programmed, and hence more robotlike, by definition. It isn't difficult to see that this type of epistemological preprogramming is the very antithesis of what it means to be truly human.

This is why we can assert that God cannot properly give us any knowledge that we can possibly gain for ourselves: because our underlying essence seems to *require* that we gain as much of our knowledge and development on our own as we possibly can. However, it is also clear that, given our prior God-given ability for self-attained growth and development, we *can* gain the vast majority of our knowledge and development on our own, through our own free-willed behavior in the world. This being the case, it is no wonder that we are initially born into such a naive and undeveloped state of being: because this is where we *necessarily* must start if our underlying purpose in life is to gain as much of our knowledge and development on our own as possible.

John Hick agrees that rational human saints could never have been created ready-made to begin with, even by an omnipotent Creator, and he appeals to the intrinsic value of self-attained virtue to prove his point:

The first stage of the creative process was, to our anthropomorphic imaginations, easy for divine omnipotence. By an exercise of creative power God caused the physical universe to exist, and in the course of countless ages to bring forth within it organic life, and finally to produce out of organic life personal life; and when man had thus emerged out of the evolution of the forms of organic life, a creature had been made who has the possibility of existing in conscious fellowship with God. But the second stage of the creative of the creative process is of a different kind altogether. *It cannot be performed by omnipotent power as such.* For personal life is essentially free and self-directing. It cannot be perfected by divine fiat, but only through the uncompelled responses and willing co-operation of human individuals in their actions and reactions in the world in which God has placed them. Men may eventually become the perfected persons whom the New Testament calls children of God', but they cannot be created ready-made as this.

The value-judgement that is implicitly being invoked here is that one who has attained to goodness by meeting and eventually mastering temptations, and thus by rightly making responsible choices in concrete situations, is good in a richer and more valuable sense than would be one created *ab initio* in a state of either innocence or virtue. In the former case, which is that of the actual moral achievements of mankind, the individual's goodness has within it the strength of temptations overcome, a stability based upon an accumulation of right choices, and a positive and responsible character that comes from the investment of costly personal effort. I suggest, then, that it is an ethically reasonable judgement, even though in the nature of the case not one that is capable of demonstrative proof, that human goodness slowly built up through personal histories of moral effort has a value in the eyes of the Creator which justifies even the long travail of the soul-making process (emphasis mine).[7]

Hick believes that humans could never have been created ready-made because he is convinced that beings who have actualized themselves through their own hard work are inherently more valuable in the eyes of God than are beings who have been created "perfect" to begin with. As to why this is the case, Hick simply states that God cannot instantaneously create free and self-directing beings by definition. And since free and self-directing beings are held to be intrinsically more valuable in the eyes of God than their instantaneously-created counterparts, it follows that God would obviously want to create this type of being only. This, according to Hick, is why we weren't created in a perfect developmental state to begin with.

It would be a mistake, however, to simply assume that self-directing humans are fundamentally similar to their ready-made counterparts once they have both been instantiated. To the contrary, self-directing humans appear to belong to a different ontological class *altogether*, since their underlying mode of creation fundamentally alters virtually every aspect of their inner experience and reality. In fact, there is such an immense gap separating these two types of beings that can call the term "ready-made human" an oxymoron, since genuine humans are allegedly *defined* as being free-willed, rational agents who must acquire their own psychospiritual development for themselves. It is thus logically impossible, on this view, for there to be an instantaneously-created human being because the very *definition* of humanity requires that there be an underlying freedom of self-direction in such an individual's life.[8]

It is for this reason that genuine human beings must be self-assembling by their very nature: because this is the only way that they can fully direct the course of their own lives on this planet. It is also the only way that they can acquire an independent and self-owned identity for themselves, because the more people struggle for their own full development, the more they can be said to "own" it in a deep existential sense.

Our necessary freedom also extends to our relationship to God as well, because the only way that we can have a real choice about whether or not we want to be committed to our Maker is if we are first created without any direct knowledge of His existence. This "epistemic distance" between God and humanity is, according to Hick, absolutely essential if our love towards God is to be genuine, because some degree of separation between God and humanity is the logically necessary precondition for free-willed personal choice as far as our devotion to God is concerned. For if we were initially created in the direct and unmitigated presence of our Creator, we would automatically be *compelled* to follow Him *no matter what*, and it is clear that compulsory allegiance doesn't qualify as real love at all.

Our creation in the direct presence of God would also have the effect of rendering us unfree in our own personal lives as well, because it would then be next to impossible for us to do as we really pleased on this planet, since in this case God would be right on top of us, as it were, indirectly intimidating us to behave in an unfree and regimented fashion. However, if we are first created in a world in which it appears as if there is no God, we can then grow and develop as we please, especially in terms of our relationship to our Maker. But then, once we become spiritually mature enough to be able to freely choose whether or not we actually want to align ourselves with our Creator, we will no longer be overwhelmed in a negative sense by His Power and Great Glory.

The upshot of this realization is simply that our world must necessarily be partially "evil" at the present time if we are to be capable of existing and growing as genuine human beings. To the extent that this assertion is accurate, it follows that God cannot be held to be morally responsible for the many evil events that take place in our world, even though He is the one who originally created this evil-prone state of affairs to begin with, because the world must *necessarily* be this way in order for us to exist.

It is this concept of a higher metaphysical necessity that acquits God of any moral culpability for evil, just as it also preserves God's omnipotence and perfect goodness in the process. Indeed, we can even go so far as to assert that God's allowance of this kind of necessary evil into the world is evidence of His great *love* for humankind, since He is evidently willing to tolerate the most unpleasant of conditions in order to give humans the genuine opportunity to exist.

Of course, this line of reasoning can only begin to make sense if God's creative power turns out to have been significantly constrained by the intrinsic nature of the Human Essence itself, such that He could not have brought about our ultimate good in any other logically possible way. But to the extent that this is indeed the case, God should never be faulted for His allowance of evil in the world; He should, rather, be *commended* for it, despite the temporary existence of evil, because this is presumably the only logically possible way there is for us to get into the kingdom. Indeed, this appears to be the sense in which we were "bought for a price" (1 Cor. 6:20). The "price" here is simply the metaphysical cost that is intrinsically required to initiate us into the kingdom.

A Developmental Interpretation of Evil

The developmental interpretation of human wickedness that we are pursuing in this book is capable of explaining two of the most confusing and mysterious views of evil that have been offered over the years. The first view, championed primarily by Augustine and Aquinas, sees evil as mainly a privation of good. On this view, evil has no substance in itself, so it is forced to feed off the good before it can fully manifest its own destructive properties. This is known as the doctrine of the *privatio boni*, and it has vigorously been upheld by traditional theologians throughout the millennia because of its consistency with the existence of a perfectly good and all-powerful Creator.

Developmentally speaking, we can identify the good that we have been deprived of *in our own personalities*, since it is the good of our own full development that has deliberately been taken away from us in order to fulfill the intrinsic demands of the Human Essence. This privation of our own full development produces evil because *anything* that is only partially assembled is prone to malfunctioning by definition, and this includes human souls. Specifically, it is the lack of an optimal amount of evil-preventing knowledge and moral development that tends to generate evil in immature humans, as we have seen.

Fortunately, though, this concept of evil as privation carries within itself the seeds of its own destruction, for once human beings become mature and responsible enough to be able to prevent evil through their own behavior, the plague of moral evil will automatically cease *by definition.* This is why we can say that the curse of moral evil is only temporary: because it is only a matter of time until we become individuated to the point that we are no longer unduly prone to behavioral malfunctioning.

The second time-honored strategy for envisioning the origin of evil is that which identifies evil with metaphysical nothingness. G.W. Leibniz has called this nebulous contribution to human wickedness "metaphysical evil," because it presumably arises from the very finiteness of our existence, which is said to interface mysteriously with the "evil abyss" of absolute nothingness. While this may true to some limited extent, it is hard to see why finiteness *qua* finiteness is able to wreak such havoc in our world, especially since many finite objects in our experience are known to be capable of functioning very precisely and admirably in the world *despite their finitude.*

A much better usage of this principle of non-being (which is also called *das Nichtige* in Karl Barth's philosophical system) locates the metaphysical nothingness, not in the nature of our surrounding environment *per se*, but rather in the ontological nature of our own souls. For if we have truly been deprived of our full development for larger teleological reasons, then it naturally follows that there must be a significant part of our character structure *that has yet to be formed.* This temporary lack of character completion is indeed a very real type of existential nothingness, because the undeveloped parts of the personality obviously haven't taken on a concrete structure for themselves yet. It is primarily in this sense that the ethereal qualities of non-being are capable of predisposing us so strongly to moral evil: because they are indicative of the extent to which our characters are still immature, and therefore prone to behavioral malfunctioning.

The ancient Greeks called this type of metaphysical nothingness "meontic non-being," which can be defined as the negatively positive or positively negative form of non-being that has the potential of turning into something real. It was distinguished from absolute non-being or blank nothingness, which has no potential to turn into anything at all. Meontic non-being thus can be seen to exist in our own partially developed souls, which clearly have the potential of turning into something real when they finally become "filled in" by a more mature personality structure in the future.[9]

It follows from this realization that Leibniz probably confused the developmental aspects of our own *internal* non-being for the metaphysical nature of non-being in general. This distinction is critical, because it transfers the locus of metaphysical necessity in the universe from the nature of generic reality itself to the specific nature of a particular essence, namely that of human beings. This movement has profound philosophical and theological

Evil in the Old Testament 115

repercussions, both for our conceptualization of the Divine Power as well as for our understanding of the ultimate genesis of moral evil.

Notes

1. John A. Sanford, *Evil: The Shadow Side of Reality*, pp. 26–27.
2. C.S. Lewis, *God in the Dock*, Walter Hooper, ed. (Grand Rapids: Eerdmans, 1970), p. 22.
3. Please refer to Bruce Reichenback's *Evil and a Good God* (pp. 87–118) and Richard Swinburne's *The Existence of God* (pp. 203–204) for two compelling theodicies of natural evil.
4. John A. Sanford, *Evil: The Shadow Side of Reality*, p. 27.
5. David Ray Griffin, in *Encountering Evil*, Stephen T. Davis, ed. (Atlanta: John Knox Press, 1981), pp. 106–109.
6. While this metaphysical principle does indeed seem to apply to all possible worlds, it *still* doesn't qualify as a genuine explanation for the existence of evil, because it begs the true question that is at issue here, which is this: why can't intrinsically valuable beings always use their power for the exclusive attainment of good? It is thus beside the point that these intrinsically valuable beings have the *potential* power for good or evil, because the real problem pertains exclusively to why they are *actually* unable to use their power to bring about the good *only*. The answer to this question has nothing directly to do with the amount of potential power that these beings possess; it instead points back to their internal character deficits that make destructive personal choices more likely to happen overall. These deficits include a general lack of practical knowledge about how to bring about the good, as well as an internal moral deficiency that results in a lack of desire to want to do the good in all possible circumstances. *These* are the true reasons why we are so prone to doing evil, and while it is certainly correct to say that we wouldn't be capable of doing so much evil if we weren't also capable of doing so much good, it is also true that our potential for evil could have forever remained a potentiality only, via the exclusive actualization of the good in all circumstances. Something obviously prevented this alleged possibility from being realized at the beginning of human history; nevertheless, the concept of heaven *requires* that this possibility be fully realized in the distant future, when we are presumably going to be morally and epistemologically developed enough to be able to produce only good with our behavior.
7. Ibid., pp. 255–256.
8. Hick implicitly seems to assume the validity of this essentialistic terminology, but he cleverly avoids explicitly mentioning it in his writing, presumably because of the highly contentious nature of essentialism in modern philosophy.
9. I don't mean to imply that our quest for optimal character development represents a static, and therefore fully obtainable, goal. To the contrary, it appears as though we will continue learning and growing for eternity, which means that we will probably never reach an *absolute* level of full character development. However, it is still possible for us to eventually reach a level of *relative* completion, which will take place when we become developed enough to be able to avoid any further production of evil with our own behavior.

CHAPTER FIVE
Answer to Jung

C.G. Jung's *Answer to Job* is one of the most in-depth psychological studies of the book of Job ever written. It probes many of the nuances of orthodox theological tradition through the use of an emotional writing style that is highly amenable to the lay reader.

Dr. Jung's self-professed purpose in writing this intriguing book was twofold. First, he wanted to explore his many deep-seated feelings about the type of God found in the Old Testament, and secondly, he wanted to obtain insight into the religious problem of evil by using the various analytical tools that he had developed during his professional study of psychology. The results of his labor are both interesting and highly contentious, and they are very much of interest to anyone who is interested in the often perplexing relationship between psychology and religion. It will therefore serve us well in our psychological study of Job to examine Jung's ideas in depth.

Jung and the God of the Old Testament

Jung takes a very critical view of the Deity who is portrayed in the book of Job. Going against the grain of orthodox religious tradition, Jung chooses to blame God for all the evils that have befallen the hapless Job. He even goes so far as to argue that God was somehow morally inferior to the upright Job, which presumably explains why He tried to destroy Job altogether through the evil machinations of Satan. Evidently Jung believed that God was so unconscious and morally imperfect that He felt compelled to completely do away with His creature Job, since the latter ironically seemed to constitute the single greatest threat to God's position of Absolute Moral Authority in the universe.

It comes as no surprise, then, that Jung concentrates almost exclusively on God's wounding of Job without apparent cause (Job 9:17). Jung wants to know why a good God would do such a terrible thing, when He is supposed to represent perfect love and not blind destructiveness. Indeed, since Jung takes Job's protestations of innocence at face value, he places the ultimate blame for Job's suffering squarely on God Himself, for allowing Satan to deliver so much wrath to Job without just cause. In accordance with this radical position, Jung believes that Satan "bamboozled" God into devastating an innocent man because of God's own lack of consciousness.[1] A morally conscious Deity, Jung argues, would have seen to it that Job was treated with more reverence.

The chief weakness in Jung's interpretation lies in his belief that Job's wounds were multiplied without cause. This statement should be updated to read "without *apparent* cause." It is one thing to remark that Job's wounds were multiplied by God for no apparent cause, and quite another to remark that they were multiplied for no real cause at all. For how could Jung (or anyone else for that matter) possibly know whether or not Job's wounds were multiplied by God without true cause? While Job repeatedly proclaimed his innocence, this doesn't necessarily mean that he was really and truly innocent, since many people who are accused of wrongdoing routinely proclaim their innocence to the rest of the world.

What we *do* know for a certainty about Job is that he was a man who was in the ongoing process of character development. As such, he was undoubtedly subject to the same sorts of problems that we are all naturally subject to. While he may not have outwardly acted in a destructive manner, this doesn't necessarily mean that he was truly blameless on the inside. After all, who knows what kinds of spiritual evils were lurking about deep inside of Job's unconscious? Indeed, the Pharisees of Jesus' time were the most well-behaved people in their society, since they outwardly obeyed every letter of the Law, yet inwardly they were "full of dead men's bones and everything unclean" (Matt. 23:27). As a consequence, they were severely reprimanded for their hypocrisy by our Lord, who more than once declared that God looks into the innermost heart of man, instead of merely to his outer behavior.

Why Bad Things Happen to Good People

The problem of why bad things happen to good people has been of paramount importance throughout human history. Most people evidently think of themselves as being good, yet just about everyone ends up suffering more in their lives than they think they deserve to. The Bible, however, disputes this self-perception of goodness because it tells us that *all* human beings are sinful, and so fall short of the glory of God (Rom. 3:23). To the extent that this is so, we find that no one is immune from suffering because of any amount of self-perceived goodness. In fact, if suffering is temporarily a necessary part of the human condition, and furthermore, if it is a necessary "propellant" for our continued spiritual growth, we must conclude that both "good" and "bad" people alike need to suffer, since suffering is, on this view, the only Divinely-prescribed way there is for human beings to achieve their goal of full character growth for themselves.

Indeed, we have seen how our outer goodness isn't always a reliable indicator of our true inner state, because it could merely be an appearance only, and as such it could end up providing a potent stumbling block to our ongoing quest for the kingdom. More than once Jesus declared that "many of the first will be last, and the last first" (Matt. 19:30, Luke 13:30). We can take this enigmatic saying to mean that many of the traditional outer markers for success will be negatively correlated with our progress towards self-actualization, such that the more "successful" we are in our worldly lives, the less mature and developed we will tend to be on the inside, and vice versa. The reason for this inscrutable state of affairs has to do with the paradoxical nature of spiritual growth, which in many cases is directly incompatible with worldly success because of the radically different value system that it exemplifies. This is why many of those who are first in this world in terms of their worldly success will be last in the next world: because their opulent lifestyle will have prevented them from growing spiritually to any significant degree, and it is precisely this type of spiritual growth that is the chief prerequisite for a better life beyond the grave. By the same token, many of those who are last in this world in terms of materialistic success will be first in the next world, because their spiritually-oriented value system will have enabled them to grow into a better life after they die.

The life of Jesus perfectly exemplified this paradoxical spiritual principle, because He was one of the most spiritually developed human beings of all time, yet He was a complete and total failure as far as the traditional society of His time was concerned. Jesus would have been even more of a failure today than He was 2000 years ago, because as far as our modern system of materialistic values is concerned, He would have been considered little more than a homeless and unemployed bum.

The point is simply that our fitness for the kingdom isn't determined by how good we are in an outer sense, or by how much "success" we happen to experience in our day-to-day lives. It is, rather, determined by the degree to which we are able to individuate in this world. This is why suffering in the here-and-now is such an important factor in determining our fate in the next life: because suffering is a far more potent catalyst for growth than raw pleasure is, which explains why suffering is the central paradigm around which many of the world's major religions are based. As Jesus tells us, we absolutely *must* pick up our own personal cross and follow Him if we are to be counted as true Christians. But this means voluntarily experiencing the *profound* suffering of the cross, no matter how unpleasant it may be.

In the following quote from *Reason and Religion*, John Hick gives an excellent explanation of why meaningful spiritual growth could never happen in a hedonistic paradise:

> Man could not develop morally and spiritually in a paradise. The best of all possible worlds for his present comfort and pleasure might well be the worst of all possible worlds for his growth into a higher quality of existence.

Moral and spiritual growth are not spontaneous but come in response to challenges, in the making of choices, in the facing of difficulties and problems, and through the coping with setbacks and failures as well as enjoying success and achievement. Hence something like our present imperfect world, with its contingencies and uncertainties, is an environment more apt for person making than would be a stress-free paradise.[2]

Jesus further hints at this paradoxical relationship between suffering and the kingdom when he forgives the woman of ill repute who is truly sorry for her sins (Luke 7:36–50). Although the Pharisees reproach Him for His endorsement of such a known sinner, Jesus corrects them by pointing out that those who are forgiven little love little, and that those who are forgiven much love much (Luke 7:47). This woman undoubtedly suffered a great deal in response to her sinful life, which explains why Jesus chose to forgive her: because her suffering probably led to a substantial amount of spiritual growth on the inside, which in turn would have enabled her to love others more than she would have otherwise been able to do.

Elsewhere Jesus even goes so far as to say that prostitutes and tax collectors will be getting into the kingdom before many of the Church's holiest members will (Matt. 21:31). The reasoning here is the same as that found in the previous example, for it is only by suffering tremendously that people can grow to the point that they are intrinsically fit for the kingdom. More often than not, however, it the most sinful members of society (i.e., the "last") who end up suffering such an extreme amount, which explains why they are getting into the kingdom first. The more "privileged" members of society, on the other hand, are much more shielded from the refining effects of pain and suffering, so they presumably aren't individuating very much, which in turn explains why they aren't getting into the kingdom as quickly.

A Pluralistic View of Salvation

Before we move on, a brief word needs to be said about the relevance of the world's other major religions to the psychospiritual message being forwarded in this book. For although I am focusing primarily on the Christian religion in this text, I believe that all of the relevant spiritual principles that are outlined herein are equally applicable to *all* of the world's major religions. In this sense I regard the world's three great monotheistic religions, Judaism, Christianity, and Islam, to be fundamentally similar, insofar as all three worship the same Creator and all three promote the same type of moral development in the individual. While many fundamentalist Christians would prefer to argue for the absolute exclusivity of Christian salvation, I believe that the redemptive spirit of Christ is implicit in *anyone* who sincerely worships the Creator, regardless of the identity of the larger religion that he or she happens to be following. This belief has the advantage of making salvation accessible to all those individuals who happened to live before the time of Christ, as well as to those who have never heard of Him today, and it is also entirely consistent with the teaching of the Bible on this controversial subject as well (Rom. 2:12–16).

So, while I personally believe in the absolute Deity of Christ, I also believe that it is possible for anyone to be an "anonymous Christian" by following the instinctual rules of salvation that have been written into each human heart, as the second chapter of Romans clearly explains:

But because of your stubbornness and your unrepentant heart, you are storing up wrath against yourself for the day of God's wrath, when his righteous judgment will be revealed. God "will give to each person according to what he has done." To those who by persistence in doing good seek glory, honor and immortality, he will give eternal life. But for those who are self-seeking and who reject the truth and follow evil, there will be wrath and anger. There will be trouble and distress for every human being who does evil: first for the Jew, then for the Gentile; ıbut glory, honor and peace for everyone who does good: first for the Jew, then for the Gentile. For God does not show favoritism.

All who sin apart from the law will also perish apart from the law, and all who sin under the law will be judged by the law. ıFor it is not those who hear the law who are righteous in God's sight, but it is those who obey the law who will be declared righteous. (Indeed, when Gentiles, who do not have the law, do by nature things required by the law, they are a law for themselves, even though they do not have the law, since they show that the requirements of the law are written on their hearts, their consciences also bearing witness, and their thoughts now accusing, now even defending them.) This will take place on the day when God will judge men's secrets through Jesus Christ, as my gospel declares (Rom. 2:5–16).

This is the way of truthful life that Jesus personified, which means that it can be followed by anyone anywhere who sincerely desires to change for the better. But sincerely follow it one must, because there is no salvation to be had *anywhere* that does not exemplify this Christ-like principle of psychological redemption. This is the indirect sense in which no one comes to the Father except through Jesus (John 14:6). The basic idea here is that no one can be saved apart from the way of truthful living that was personified by Christ's life, because this is the only road that leads to our species-based goal of individuation, which is what makes the eventual redemption of the personality possible in the first place.

Jung's View of Job

Getting back to the story of Job, we can regard Job's proclamation of absolute innocence as little more than flagrant self-deception, because it is clear that as an ordinary human being, Job wasn't yet fit enough for the kingdom, even though he clearly wasn't a wicked sinner in terms of his daily behavior. This means that he was probably in need of redemptive suffering just as much as anyone else, yet his formerly wonderful lifestyle undoubtedly prevented him from experiencing much of this necessary pain.

The point is that even the most guilt-free among us must suffer, because even the guilt-free are in need of individuation, and individuation only comes to those who suffer. This is the whole point of the cross, for if we suffer until either our physical body dies or until the evil parts of our inner selves die, we too will presumably be resurrected into a glorious state of heightened character development, not in response to any external perfecting power *per se*, but rather in response to *our own* self-motivated behaviors.

We see, then, that Dr. Jung greatly overestimated the innocence of Job, and so *underestimated* Job's need to suffer in order to be fit for the kingdom. In the process he also unduly overemphasized God's moral guilt and intrinsic degree of wickedness.

One of Job's comforters, Elihu the Buzite, effectively counters this type of blasphemous thinking by proclaiming God's absolute innocence and justice to Job:

"It is unthinkable that God would do wrong, that the Almighty would pervert justice. Who appointed him over the Earth? Who put him in charge of the whole world? If it were his intention [to do man harm], and he withdrew his spirit and breath, all mankind would perish together and man would return to the dust" (Job 34:12–15).

This is a remarkable statement that is full of insight regarding the nature of the Divine Being. For given God's definition as the most perfect being in all of existence, as well as His sole position as the undisputed Ruler of the heavens, it is unthinkable that He would do wrong and pervert justice. Indeed, if this were ever the case, none of us would stand a chance in this life, as Elihu the Buzite correctly points out. In such a pessimistic scenario, God could simply withdraw His ordering Spirit from the realm of the physical and the entire universe would instantly collapse into non-being. Hence, the very fact that we exist in a coherent world and have some concept of good and evil constitutes powerful evidence that God *must* intend us only good, and that the origin of evil must therefore be sought elsewhere.

The facts of modern cosmology support us on this point, for we now know that our existence on this planet is only possible because of an incredibly unlikely concatenation of cosmic coincidences that seem for all the world to be aimed at making the earth a habitable place for us to live.[3] There thus seems to be little doubt that had God wanted to do us gratuitous harm on this planet, He never would have created such a stable and hospitable world to begin with.

Surprisingly enough, Dr. Jung fails to find any possible goodness in God's treatment of Job. Instead, he finds it amazing:

> ... to see how easily Yahweh, quite without reason, had let himself be influenced by one of his sons [Satan], by a doubting thought, and made unsure of Job's faithfulness. With his touchiness and suspiciousness the mere possibility of doubt was enough to infuriate him and induce that peculiar double-faced behavior of which He had already given proof in the Garden of Eden, when he pointed out the tree to the First Parents and at the same time forbade them to eat of it. In this way He precipitated the Fall, which he apparently never intended. Similarly, his faithful servant Job is now to be exposed to a rigorous moral test, quite gratuitously and to no purpose, although Yahweh is convinced of Job's faithfulness and constancy, and could moreover have assured himself beyond all doubt on this point had he taken counsel with his own omniscience. Why, then, is the experiment made at all, and a bet with the unscrupulous slanderer settled, without a stake, on the back of a powerless creature? It is indeed no edifying spectacle to see how quickly Yahweh abandons his faithful servant to the evil spirit and lets him fall without compunction or pity into the abyss of physical and moral suffering. From the human point of view Yahweh's behaviour is so revolting that one has to ask oneself whether there is not a deeper motive hidden behind it. Has Yahweh some secret resistance against Job? That would explain his yielding to Satan.[4]

It is highly presumptuous for Jung to assert, as he does in the above passage, that God allowed Job to suffer gratuitously, and without purpose. There is, of course, no way to know for a certainty whether or not God in fact had a larger purpose in allowing Satan to buffet Job so intensely. But what we *do* know is that the story of Job was probably *not* meant to be taken in such a literal fashion. It was, rather, almost certainly meant to be taken allegorically, as a literary paradigm for the many existential dilemmas that characterize human existence. To the extent that this is indeed the case, it would be a grievous hermeneutic error to take the story line of Job in such a literal fashion. The fact that C.G. Jung, the father of modern symbolic thought, has persisted in doing so anyway is surely one of the greatest ironies in the entire history of philosophical theology.

The Power of Doubt

Interestingly enough, a doubting thought is all that was necessary to set into motion the cataclysmic events of Job's life, but this really isn't so surprising when we view it in terms of our day-to-day experience in this world, because doubting thoughts can easily ruin *anyone* by initiating a chain reaction of destructive behavioral events that culminate in personal disaster. Each individual personality, of course, is constantly being tried by the stresses and strains of human existence, such that any significant degree of personal doubt will surely be exploited in a negative sense by the natural course of events in our lives. This being the case, there *had* to have been a doubting thought in God's Mind about Job's blamelessness, because Job was by no means perfect from a Divine point of view.

Jung further faults God for not consulting His omniscience about the innocence of Job before allowing Satan to go on his destructive rampage. Jung is clearly assuming that Job is 100 percent innocent here, so he thinks it is ridiculous for an omniscient Being (Yahweh) to punish such a blameless person, when He should have known full well that Job was really innocent. This is why Jung believes that Yahweh is partially unconscious, but this is even more preposterous, because it is impossible *by definition* for an omniscient Being to be less than omniscient at any given time.

In one sense, though, Jung is right: it *is* absurd for an omniscient Being to deliberately punish an innocent person because of a lack of knowledge about his innocence. On the other hand, what if this individual isn't really so innocent after all, or what if his sufferings aren't literally being meted out by God? In either (or both) of these instances, God cannot be faulted for His failure to consult His omniscience because He wouldn't be guilty of committing a mistake.

Put another way, God's awareness of Job's relative degree of guilt does *not* appear to be the central question that is at issue here. Rather, it is Job's own developmental progress that is the ultimate object of his suffering, because God in His omniscience clearly knew beforehand how Job would respond to his many calamities. *This instrumental perspective completely exonerates God of any failure to consult His omniscience in His treatment of Job.*

Indeed, if we assume that God allowed Satan (as a personification of the world's own natural destructiveness) to test Job, not as a punishment for sin *per se*, but as an occasion for Job's own psychospiritual growth, we then find that an all-knowing Creator *can* in fact allow bad things to happen to good people, even though He knows full well, *via* His omniscience, how these people will respond to their suffering in the end. For while God may be aware of this eventual result, we human beings do not know, so these events must happen anyway for *our own* developmental benefit. This explains why God would have commanded Abraham to sacrifice his beloved son Isaac, even though He knew beforehand how Abraham was going to respond in the end. For while God knew how Abraham was going to respond,

Abraham himself did *not* know, so this Divine command was necessary to push Abraham to new levels of psychospiritual development.

This instrumental principle also explains why God allows us to be tested by the natural course of events in our lives, even though He knows beforehand how we are going to respond: because we in our developmental ignorance do *not* know. As a consequence, God allows us to suffer in our lives so we can grow ever closer towards our developmental goal, even though He presumably knows beforehand how we are going to turn out in the end.

This also explains why Satan is allowed to buffet Job with one curse after another. For insofar as Satan is merely a personification of the many destructive events that naturally happen to us in our lives, it stands to reason that all of us, including the most righteous among us, will naturally suffer from destructive events from time to time, some in response to our own fault-filled behaviors, and others in response to random evils that are largely beyond our control.

From this point of view, we can see how the whimsical side of Satan's torment of Job might be symbolic of those random evils that occur with no rhyme or reason behind them. Although much of our suffering undoubtedly occurs in direct karmic response to the wrong things that we have done in our lives, a great deal also occurs by chance alone. For instance, an innocent bystander might get accidentally struck down by a wayward bullet, or a family might inadvertently be killed when an airplane accidentally crashes into their home. In such instances, no clearly discernible reason for our suffering can be traced to our behavior. It happens "on its own," so to speak, in response to the type of world that God has created for us to live in.

C.S. Lewis has persuasively argued that this sort of danger-filled world is an essential prerequisite of human freedom, because we can allegedly be free only in a stable and neutral environment that is ruled by immutable physical laws. Unfortunately, given this neutral environment, it is inevitable that certain forces will operate in a destructive fashion upon those individuals who happen to be in the wrong place at the wrong time. In such instances, it is clear that God cannot miraculously alter the lawfulness of the material realm without destabilizing the entire world order, as Lewis so eloquently explains in the following passage:

> Society . . . implies a common field or "world" in which its members meet. . . . But if matter is to serve as a neutral field it must have a fixed nature of its own. If a "world" or material system had only a single inhabitant it might conform at every moment to his wishes—"trees for his sake would crowd into a shade." But if you were introduced into a world which thus varied at my every whim, you would be quite unable to act in it and would thus lose the exercise of your free will. . . .

Yet again, if the fixed nature of matter prevents it from being always, and in all its dispositions, equally agreeable to even a single soul, much less is it possible for the matter of the universe at any given moment to be distributed so that it is equally convenient and pleasurable to each member of a society. . . . If even a pebble lies where I want it to lie, it cannot, except by coincidence, be where you want it to lie. And this is very far from being an evil: on the contrary, it furnishes occasion for all those acts of courtesy, respect, and unselfishness by which love and good humour and modesty express themselves. But it certainly leaves the way open to a great evil, that of competition and hostility. And if souls are free, they cannot be prevented from dealing with the problem by competition instead of courtesy. And once they have advanced to actual hostility, they can then exploit the fixed nature of matter to hurt one another. . . .

We can, perhaps, conceive of a world in which God corrected the results of this abuse of free will by His creatures at every moment: so that a wooden beam became soft as grass when it was used as a weapon, and the air refused to obey me if I attempted to set up in it the sound waves that carry lies or insults. But such a world would be one in which wrong actions were impossible, and in which, therefore, freedom of the will would be void; nay if the principle were carried out to its logical conclusion, evil thoughts would be impossible, for the cerebral matter which we use in thinking would refuse its task when we attempted to frame them. All matter in the neighbourhood of a wicked man would be liable to undergo unpredictable alterations. That God can and does, on occasions, modify the behaviour of matter and produce what we call miracles, is part of the Christian faith; but the very conception of a common, and therefore, stable, world, demands that these occasions should be extremely rare. . . . So it is with the life of souls in a world: fixed laws, consequences unfolding by causal necessity, the whole natural order, are at once the limits within which their common life is confined and also the sole condition under which any such life is possible. *Try to exclude the possibility of suffering which the order of nature and the existence of free wills involve, and you find that you have excluded life itself* (emphasis mine).[5]

We see, then, that many types of natural evils are built into the very nature of our soul-building world. This is the part of the general world order that Satan seems to represent in the book of Job.

Once again, though, this shouldn't be taken to mean that Satan is *directly* responsible for causing human suffering in the world. The Biblical figure of Satan, as we have seen, seems to represent those naturally-occurring evils that occur to us on a daily basis, so it would be wrong to surmise that these evils are being caused by an extraterrestrial creature named Satan. It would therefore be a mistake to conclude that the story of Job teaches that all destructive events are directly caused by spiritual beings in high places. It merely teaches that: a) destructive events happen in response to naturalistic forces that are built into our current world order, and b) that once they occur, we should do our best to grow beyond them to the greatest possible extent.

In other words, we can understand the Biblical figure of Satan to be a personification for *any* type of destructive action, even those that happen naturalistically. This explains why Satan's actions are so frivolously motivated: because a great many evils in our world happen randomly, with no higher reason for their occurrence as far as each individual human being is concerned.

There is, however, an indirect "reason" for the occurrence of these random evils that applies to everyone collectively: it gives us the opportunity to issue an effective moral response to them, so we can eventually grow beyond them. For if good and evil were precisely meted out in direct response to what we do in our lives, we would be motivated to enact the good primarily for the reward we would get, and not for any higher moral reason *per se*. In such a world genuine morality would be impossible, as John Hick has astutely pointed out:

> All manner of accidents and misfortune strike randomly and therefore unjustly, without relation to human desert. But suppose that instead they occurred justly and therefore nonrandomly, so that the evil were always punished and the virtuous rewarded. Such a system would not serve a person making purpose. As Kant pointed out in his *Critique of Practical Reason* (Pt. I, Bk. II, sec. 9), it would undermine the moral life, since men would then act rightly for hope of reward or fear of punishment. In other words, moral responsibility and hence moral growth require a world in which there are genuine contingencies which distribute good and bad fortune not on the basis of desert.[6]

We see, then, that there is indeed a larger reason why a benevolent Creator would allow good and evil to strike randomly in our world. But if this is so, then God cannot be held to be morally indictable for allowing Satan to pummel Job with random evils. For insofar as the figure of Satan represents the natural course of destructive events in the world, we find that his actions in the book of Job are merely symbolic of the morality-building natural evils that strike randomly in human society.[7]

In other words, God really isn't up there deciding, along with Satan, who is going to suffer on this planet and who isn't. In actuality, this unsavory task is probably being performed by some level of interplay between randomness and the Law of Natural Causation, which of course leaves God completely out of the whole affair, except insofar as He was originally responsible for creating the entire natural order to begin with. But again, the world was presumably created in this fashion for our own ultimate benefit, because no other logically possible alternative was available for God to choose from. To the extent that this is so, it takes God completely off the hook as far as the present existence of evil is concerned.

The Severity of the Developmenal Process

In any discussion of the problem of evil, the question always arises about God's routine use of such severe measures to promote the growth of human beings, when presumably less intense measures would have had the same result. It is far from clear, however, that less severe measures would have indeed produced the same result, and the reason for this isn't far to seek, for if most humans really do harbor a number of well-entrenched obstacles to their own further development deep inside their innermost souls, then nothing less than a truly *catastrophic* series of evils will typically suffice to get rid of them. Again, this is the ultimate meaning of Christ's crucifixion on the cross. Jesus suffered so intensely during His execution in order to teach us that we too need to suffer *equally* horrible tortures before we can be capable of conquering the inner evils that bar our future progress towards individuation. Indeed, had less potent evils been able to suffice in this capacity, Jesus almost certainly would have suffered an easier means of punishment.

No one was more aware of this aspect of Christian discipleship than the German theologian Dietrich Bonhoeffer, who tragically died at the hands of the Nazis just a few days before the end of World War II. Bonhoeffer recognized that the cross is *not* a substitute for our own suffering, as many Christians today seem to think; it is, to the contrary, a Divine prescription *for* the very same type of suffering that Christ experienced during His passion. This is a tall order, to be sure, but there is no escaping the fact that "the cross means sharing the suffering of Christ to the last and to the fullest. Only a man thus totally committed in discipleship can experience the meaning of the cross."[8]

Bonhoeffer goes on to argue that "the cross is laid on every Christian. . . . As we embark upon discipleship we surrender ourselves to Christ in union with his death—we give over our lives to death. Thus it begins; the cross is not the terrible end to an otherwise god-fearing and happy life, but it meets us at the beginning of our communion with Christ. When Christ calls a man, he bids him come and die."[9]

According to Bonhoeffer, then, God's grace doesn't deliver us *away* from suffering; it rather delivers us *to* it, to the unimaginable death of the cross, because "the disciple is not above his master. Following Christ means *passio passiva*, suffering because we have to suffer."[10] Anything less Bonhoeffer calls "cheap grace," because it amounts to a justification of sin without an accompanying justification of the sinner:

> Cheap grace is the grace we bestow on ourselves. [It] . . . is the preaching of forgiveness without requiring repentance, baptism without church discipline, Communion without confession, absolution without personal confession. Cheap grace is grace without discipleship, grace without the cross, grace without Jesus Christ, living and incarnate.
>
> Costly grace is the treasure hidden in the field; for the sake of it a man will gladly go and sell all that he has. It is the pearl of great price to buy which the merchant will sell all his goods. . . . Costly grace is the gospel which must be *sought* again and again, the gift which must be *asked* for, the door at which a man must *knock*. Such grace is *costly* because it calls us to follow, and it is grace because it calls us to follow Jesus Christ. It is costly because it costs a man his life, and it is grace because it gives a man the only true life. It is costly because it condemns sin, and grace because it justifies the sinner.[11]

The moral of the story, as far as psychology is concerned, is that we mustn't underestimate the profound intractability of our inner impediments to growth just because we don't like to suffer. For as any competent psychiatrist will readily attest, these neurotic barriers are so deeply ingrained in our innermost personalities that only the most heroic of evils will *ever* succeed in rooting them out once and for all, because these are the events that force us to suffer in the same way Christ did.

Lest the reader resist this conclusion because of its seemingly exaggerated nature, it should be pointed out that modern psychology has documented the ubiquitous existence of these hard-core psychological evils within the human mind. And while it may be possible to live and act "normally" in the world in spite of these inner handicaps, it is *impossible* for us to fully individuate as long as they continue to exist within us. This explains why Jesus was so adamantly in favor of a complete spiritual cleansing for everyone: because we are *all* tainted with these inner developmental barriers to one degree or another. Unfortunately, these barriers are so deeply ingrained that nothing less than a truly hellish experience appears to be potent enough to get rid of them.

Could God Have Done Better?

In one of his most radical conclusions in *Answer to Job*, Dr. Jung states that an omnipotent God could have done a better job overall in His creation of human beings, whom he likens to "bad earthenware pots."[12] Such an assertion, however, is by no means self-evident, because not even an omnipotent God could have created significantly free human persons instantaneously, as we have seen, since such an act would have necessarily entailed that He violate their freedom through the preprogramming of their minds.

But if this is true, then at least on this one point God obviously could *not* have done a better job when He created humanity.

Unfortunately, Jung does not perceive this essential truth. For some reason (probably having to do with the current existence of evil in the world), Jung feels compelled to believe that an omnipotent God could indeed have done a better job when He created the world. This leads Jung to regard God's creation of fallible human beings as a mistake, and he even goes so far as to attribute God's many bouts of anger with the human race to His extreme frustration over this unprecedented blunder!

Jung further faults God for repeatedly demanding praise and adulation from His human subjects. A self-sufficient Creator, it is true, has no real need for human worship, at least not for its own sake. Everything changes, however, if we change our perspective from the Creator to the creature. For while praise may not be directly required by God, it *is* needed by human beings for *their* own growth and well-being. This is because the more we are able to respect and praise our Creator, the less proud we will end up being overall, and less pride almost always translates into a greater capacity for meaningful self-development. Moreover, since God wants us to grow as much as we possibly can towards our own full development, it follows that He wants us to praise and respect Him, not for His own vain need, but for *our own* developmental good.

Jung, however, makes the mistake of assuming that God needs this adulation, not so much for His own well-being as for His own self-awareness. He is able to make such a bizarre claim because he believes that humans are metaphysically necessary to enable God to be aware of His own existence:

> The character thus revealed fits a personality who can only convince himself that he exists through his relation to an object. Such dependence on the object is absolute when the subject is totally lacking in self-reflection and therefore has no insight into himself. It is as if he existed only by reason of the fact that he has an object which assures him that he is really there . . . Loudly as his power resounds through the universe, the basis of its existence is correspondingly slender, for it needs conscious reflection in order to exist in reality. Existence is only real when it is conscious to somebody. That is why the Creator needs conscious man even though, from sheer unconsciousness, he would like to prevent him from becoming conscious.[13]

It is difficult to see where Jung came up with this heretical concept regarding God's metaphysical dependence upon human beings. For one thing, only God alone has been alive from all eternity. This follows directly from God's own intrinsic definition. But if this is true, then God could not possibly have relied upon human beings for a knowledge of His own existence, because we didn't arrive on the scene until a relatively short time ago. The only way to escape this conclusion is to assert that God was somehow not conscious of His own existence until humans were actually created, but this seems ridiculous in the extreme.

It is also hard to see how God could have ever needed to bolster His own self-awareness to begin with, because an omniscient Being is fully self-aware by definition. But perhaps Jung merely means to say here that humans are only necessary for *improving* the state of God's consciousness, and not for making it metaphysically possible. But alas, this too is incoherent, because an omniscient and omnipotent state of mind cannot be improved upon to any significant degree. Jung seems to have forgotten that God is a perfect Being *by definition*, so He doesn't need anyone or anything to fulfill any inherent need inside of Him. Therefore, Jung's comment that "existence is real only when it is conscious to somebody" cannot possibly apply to God. It doesn't even clearly apply to human beings, because if you or I were the only living consciousness in the entire world, we would still know that we existed. Déscartes would have agreed with this point, because he never cited the existence of other self-conscious souls as proof of his own existence; he merely used the reality of *his own* subjective thought to prove to himself that he exists: *cogito, ergo, sum*. Indeed, the whole point of self-consciousness is that self-conscious beings don't need any other conscious beings in order to be self-aware, because they are aware of themselves *by definition*. And if this is true for mere mortals, then it must also be true for God Himself, who is superior to us in every conceivable way.

Moreover, it is very hard to see how God could possibly be dependent upon anyone or anything else in order to be complete. After all, the very definition of God automatically renders Him the most perfect and self-sufficient of all conceivable beings, so such a being could not possibly be dependent upon mere mortals for anything whatsoever (except possibly for the additional edification that might be obtained through the sharing of His consciousness with other independent persons).

Jung even goes so far as to claim that God is blatantly unconscious, and that He is immoral because of it:

> If Yahweh, as we would expect of a sensible human being, were really conscious of himself, he would, in view of the true facts of the case, at least have put an end to the panegyrics on his justice. But he is too unconscious to be moral. Morality presupposes consciousness. By this I do not mean to say that Yahweh is imperfect or evil, like a gnostic demiurge. He everything in its totality; therefore, among other things, he is total justice, and also its total opposite. At least this is the way he must be conceived if one is to form a unified picture of his character.[14]

This is doctrinal heresy by almost any theologian's book. It is also logically incoherent as well, for if God is truly omniscient, as Jung clearly believes Him to be, then He automatically knows all there is to know, which means that He cannot possibly be unconscious of anything at all *by definition*. Omniscience and unconsciousness are thus two mutually exclusive states of being that cannot possibly co-exist with one another in the same entity. The fact that Jung does not seem to have been aware of this mutually contradictory state suggests that he was probably harboring some sort of deep inner bias against the God of the Old Testament.

Jung's belief that God is "everything in its totality" also seems to be patently unreasonable as well. If this were true, God would then be the most evil being in the entire universe by definition, because this is the opposite of perfect goodness. But the very concept of perfect goodness *intrinsically excludes* any type of evil whatsoever, so it is hard to see how a perfectly good Being could ever harbor even the smallest amount of evil inside Himself. The Bible strongly supports this contention, insofar as it tells us that there is no sin or evil in God at all (1 John 3:5; James 1:13).

Jung wants to get around this apparent ontological necessity by claiming that it is in the very nature of God to be an *antinomy*, or totality of inner opposites. But it is hard to see how or why this must be the case, especially given the time-honored view of God as being the very essence of perfect love and moral perfection. Indeed, if God were even remotely evil, it is clear that none of us would stand a chance in this life, because we would constantly have to contend with an evil being who is infinitely more powerful than we will *ever* be.

For some reason, though, Jung is convinced that the only way to obtain a unified conceptualization of God's character is by proclaiming Him to be a totality of all opposites. But it is far from clear that this is indeed the case. Just because God's various qualities are said to be infinite in scope doesn't necessarily mean that they have to include all possible states of affairs. Indeed, as we have just seen, precisely the *opposite* situation seems to be true, because perfect goodness intrinsically *excludes* all forms of genuine badness by definition. *But if this is so, then God can't possibly be a constellation of fully realized opposites, because such a state is inherently contradictory, and therefore incoherent.*

Jung's persistent need to view God as an antinomy seems to originate from his intimate awareness of how the *human* mind actually works. For it is indeed the case that the human psyche contains within itself a large number of realities that are logically opposed to one another. But it would be an anthropomorphic mistake of the grandest kind if one were to project this human characteristic onto the nature of God Himself, because God is not human, that our own intrinsic qualities should apply equally to Him.

Jung also makes the critical mistake of failing to distinguish between true unreconcilable opposites, and those qualities that only *seem* to be mutually opposed to one another, but which are in fact part of the same overall polarity. In other words, although Jung claims that God is an antinomy, he fails to distinguish between ontologically true opposites, on the one hand, and merely apparent opposites, on the other. He is therefore correct to say that there appears to be a dark side to the Deity, but he is incorrect in his belief that it constitutes a genuine opposite to God's good and loving side.

In this sense Jung isn't alone. People from time immemorial have had an incredibly difficult time distinguishing apparent truth from real truth, especially with respect to the Divine nature. Human intellectual history has been fraught with a great many such errors, so we need to be constantly on guard when we are thinking about the essential nature of the Godhead, which is the most profound subject of them all. For as the Bible tells us, the ways of God are not the ways of man (Isa. 55:8). As a consequence, we have to be especially careful not to mistake our idiosyncratic prejudices for Divine truth.

It is therefore quite possible that the apparent dark side of God, which is manifested through the evil in the world, is an appearance only. This would be the case if evil were somehow a necessary ingredient in the production of the greatest possible good for humanity. In this instance, God's apparent dark side would actually be a necessary manifestation of His good and all-loving side, which in turn would mean that it isn't genuinely evil after all, since it would be subsumed under the overall rubric of the good.

The very nature of God's apparent dark side, *vis-à-vis* the human developmental journey, strongly supports this optimistic contention, because it appears as though the intrinsic necessities surrounding our own development *require* this type of negative force in order to be functional. For as John Sanford has aptly pointed out, God's dark side only destroys that which is not fit to exist in the first place.[15] This seems to make it an essential tool of the good instead of a tool of the devil. But if this is so, then God's dark side must be an illusion only, at least insofar as it isn't something that is permanently and irrevocably evil.

This sort of argument isn't as untenable as it may initially seem, because a large number of distinguished thinkers throughout history have thought along these very same lines, without contradiction or incoherence. Augustine, Aquinas, and Leibniz, for instance, all sincerely believed in this instrumental view of evil, which explains how they were able to maintain a coherent belief in a perfectly good and all-powerful Deity in spite of the world's huge surplus of evil. Indeed, this is where John Hick, Richard Swinburne, and a number of other modern theodicists have found a plausible solution to the problem of evil, *vis-à-vis* the existence of an omnipotent Creator. For as long as evil is conceived as a necessary instrument of the good, it ceases to be genuine evil in the end.

This is one of the main reasons why Jung believed that evil cannot simply be the result of a privation of good: because his worldview requires a permanent place for evil in the fourth person of the Godhead (Satan). However, the Christian doctrine of the *privatio boni* does not allow for such an enthronement of evil, since it calls for the eventual elimination of evil altogether once the good has been fully realized.

Jung was also opposed to the doctrine of the *privatio boni* because he believed that it somehow lessens our overall respect for evil, as we have seen. For if evil is truly nothing more than a parasite on the good, then it can have no real ontological existence of its own, and this in turn seems to minimize its inherent danger to us. Such an impression, however, is misleading, because a good that has been deprived of its own full goodness can be just as demonic as an evil that has an independent existence of its own, as anyone who is flying at 35,000 feet in a mechanically deficient airplane knows only too well!

Nevertheless, Jung continued to believe to the end of his life that the doctrine of the *privatio boni* is ridiculous, and would not have been necessary "had one not had to assume in advance that it is impossible for the consciousness of a good God to produce evil deeds."[16]

Such a statement is only true, however, of genuine evils, or those evils that the world would have been better off without, all things considered.[17] But the world clearly would *not* have been better off without those evils that are capable of transforming us into better people. This point becomes doubly relevant if our goal of self-actualization is not obtainable in any other way, because this possibility would enable us to fully justify God's use of an evil means to help produce a greater good in the end.

The significance of this instrumental view of evil, then, is twofold. First, it helps to preserve the absolute monotheism that the three great religions of the world—Islam, Judaism, and Christianity—have based themselves upon. For as long as evil is an independent autonomous agency opposed to God, then God's absolute sovereignty over the universe is nullified, and we are left with an unsatisfying Manichean type of dualism. However, if evil is an essential—and therefore unavoidable—component of God's quest for the greatest possible good for humanity, it then becomes an effective instrumental tool that a benevolent Creator can use to advantage to bring about good things in the world.

The second advantage of this instrumental view of evil is that it preserves God's omnipotence in the face of worldly evil. For if evil has an autonomous power independent from God, then God clearly cannot be all-powerful. On the other hand, if evil is merely an essential tool that a good God must temporarily utilize in order to bring about greater goods in the world, then it becomes logically impossible for these greater goods to be instantiated without the temporary production of evil, which in turn means that God's all-power actually ends up being preserved in the face of evil. This is because God's "inability" to bring about a contradictory state of affairs (in this case greater goods without temporary evil) doesn't constitute a genuine limitation on His all-power. John Hick agrees:

> God's all-power does not mean that He can do anything, if 'anything' is held to include self-contradictions such as making a round square, or a horse that has none of the characteristics of a horse, or an object whose surface both is and is not red all over at the same time. The self-contradictory, or logically absurd, does not fall within the scope of God's omnipotence; for a self-contradiction, being a logically meaningless form of words, does not describe anything that might be either done or not done. As Aquinas comments, 'it is more appropriate to say that such things cannot be done, than that God cannot do them.' Thus, for example, God will never make a four-sided triangle. However, this is not because He cannot make figures with four or any other number of sides, but merely because the meaning of the word 'triangle' is such that it would never be correct to call a four-sided figure a triangle. Clearly this does not involve any limitation upon God's power such that if He had greater power He would be able to accomplish these logical absurdities. Not even infinite might can adopt a meaningless form of words as a programme for action.[18]

It is this manner of reasoning that explains why privative formulations of the problem of evil have been so popular throughout the ages. The basic idea here is that as long as evil is merely conceived as a parasite upon the good, and not as a genuine ontological opposite of the good, then God's monotheistic and omnipotent nature can indeed be preserved in the face of worldly evil.

Insofar as this privative view of evil is actually correct, then, we must conclude that Jung was very much mistaken in his contention that God is partly good and partly evil. For if evil only feeds off the good, and therefore has no separate existence of its own, and if God must temporarily utilize evil forces in order to achieve the greatest possible degree of good in human affairs, then God turns out to be 100 percent good, even though evil may temporarily exist in the world. This is the aesthetic view of evil that Augustine championed over fifteen centuries ago, which states that evil is an important ingredient to the overall character of good in the world. Like a painting that utilizes dark splotches to bring out its more important elements, the world itself in this conceptualization also uses "dark splotches" (i.e., evil) to bring out *its* more important elements (i.e., the growth of fully developed human souls). We simply need to take a step back from the action so we can view individual evil events in terms of the larger whole, just as we need to look at an entire painting before the dark splotches within it begin to make sense.

It is the tremendous scope and difficulty of the human developmental process that tends to confuse us into seeing God as a totality of opposites instead of as pure goodness. If we could only see human development for what it really is—the most outrageously ambitious project in the entire history of the universe—this confusion would quickly disappear. For if it is indeed true that we are destined to be the literal offspring of the Great Creator Himself, as the Judeo-Christian tradition directly teaches, then we have set before us the most prodigious goal that we could possibly imagine, which is the internalization of some of God's most important spiritual attributes. This is apparently what the Bible means when it tells us that we were created in the image of God (Gen: 1:26–27); namely, that we are destined to share many important spiritual qualities with God Himself.

There is a problem, however, with this type of overly ambitious project: we are finite beings and God is an infinite Being. Therefore, before we can properly be created in God's spiritual image, a finite way needs to be found to mirror God's infinitude in our own souls. In some respects this appears to be an infinitely difficult task, because the "distance" between finitude and infinitude is itself infinite, as we have seen. This would seem to explain why we are having such a difficult time here on planet earth as far as the existence of evil is concerned: because we are trying to accomplish an ontological task that itself appears to be infinitely difficult.

This in turn raises another important question: what happens when an infinitely powerful being tries to accomplish a task that is itself infinitely difficult? This is similar to the time-honored question of whether God can create a stone that is too large for Him to lift. The answer, at least as far as we humans are concerned, seems to be that God *can* complete an infinitely difficult (but otherwise coherent) task, but only by "pulling out all the stops," as it were, and resorting to truly profound measures to get the job done, such as using evil means to produce greater goods.

Actually, our developmental task doesn't appear to be infinitely difficult in all respects, because we aren't expected to become truly infinite in the same way that God is. We are only expected to mirror in finite form *some* of the infinite spiritual qualities that our spiritual Father possesses. But how can this be? How can a finite spiritual being possibly mirror an infinite being in any realistic way?

One answer to this question may already be right in front of us, insofar as the very existence of our psychospiritual consciousness itself seems to have an infinite quality to it. After all, we have absolutely no idea where our conscious awareness ultimately comes from or how it really works. All we know is that we do in fact possess it, and that it enables us to do some pretty marvelous things with our minds. For instance, we can contemplate the mathematical concept of infinity and even grade the relative sizes of different types of infinities. We can also come up with mathematical descriptions of the universe that turn out to be remarkably accurate, just as we can also use our minds to probe to the very reaches of the heavens, utilizing internal mental capabilities that seem for all the world to be miraculous by their very nature. These capacities clearly seem to have some sort of infinite aspect to them, insofar as they seem to be made up of a spiritual quality that itself seems to be unbounded. Certainly our mental world (Karl Popper's World 3) is itself infinite in terms of the number of possible thoughts, forms, and images that it can come up with.

One of the reasons why finite "children of God" are so hard to create seems to be related to the inherent difficulty that is associated with making finite spiritual persons who are free and autonomous agents. God clearly cannot create this type of being ready-made, as we have seen, because to do so would necessarily violate its freedom on several different levels. To reiterate, its freedom in relation to itself would be violated by such an instantaneous creation, because it would entail the preprogramming of its entire knowledge database from the very outset, and this, in turn, would automatically transform it into a subhuman robot that could only behave the way it was originally programmed to behave. This is clearly *not* what being human is all about.

The instantaneous creation of such a preprogrammed agent would also destroy its freedom in relation to God as well, since it would have to be brought into existence in the immediate presence of its Creator. This, in turn, would eliminate its freedom to choose whether or not it wants to be close to God, just as it would also severely limit the creature's ability to freely act on its own, since the overwhelming presence of God would make it essentially impossible for it to engage in evil behaviors. Forced love, however, is clearly not what God had in Mind when He created humanity, as Hick has pointed out.[19] If it were, then we would have *already* been in God's direct presence from day one.

But if this forced allegiance isn't what God wants from us, then things immediately become much more difficult for Him. That is to say, if God really wants His human creatures to come to Him in an uncompelled free response of love and devotion, then He *cannot* compel them to do so, which means that they cannot be created in His direct presence, or even with the compulsion to love and adore Him. But this can only mean that they must be created at a certain *epistemic distance* from their Creator, for insofar as these newly-created beings are directly aware of their Maker in any significant capacity, their freedom to come to Him in an uncompelled act of love will be severely compromised. This is why it is logically impossible for an omnipotent God to instantly create beings who freely respond to Him in a loving fashion: because their instantaneous creation would simultaneously eliminate their freedom in relation to Him. This is how we can reconcile the present existence of our evil-filled world with the existence of an omnipotent Creator: because not even omnipotence itself can bring about two mutually exclusive states of affairs simultaneously.

Now we can begin to appreciate the profoundly difficult task that God set up for Himself when He opted to create finite replicas of His own Eternal Nature. The very ambitiousness of this project can be seen to have severely restricted the possible means that were available to Him to get the job done. For as we have seen, the intrinsic freedom of individual human beings is contingent upon their *not* being created ready-made. But if God cannot create humans ready-made, then the only remaining alternative is for them to create themselves (in a psychospiritual sense), through their own self-development from humble beginnings. The catch here is that this process of self-creation is fraught with all types of difficulties, because partially-assembled spiritual beings by definition do not have enough knowledge or moral development to be able to behave in a totally constructive (and therefore entirely good) manner in their day-to-day lives. This is undoubtedly why there is so much moral evil in the world: because most people simply don't know how to behave any better at this point in their self-development. If they did, they clearly wouldn't do half the things that they ordinarily do.

Socrates' famous dictum, which states that those who truly know the good cannot fail to do it, comes to mind here. Of course, this doesn't mean that most wrong-doers are totally uninformed about the wrong nature of their behavior. They obviously do have *some* idea that what they're doing is wrong. But they clearly don't have a *sufficient* knowledge of the good to prevent them from doing what they're doing; if they did, they couldn't possibly do it.

In other words, partial knowledge of the good isn't what is required here; *full* knowledge is. Unfortunately, partially-developed humans rarely have a full knowledge of the good in most instances, because if they did, they would be fully developed by definition, and this is metaphysically impossible at this early stage of our development. It is metaphysically impossible because of the extreme level of ontological sophistication that God is trying to build into us, as the following passage from Hick makes perfectly clear:

> The first stage of the creative process was, to our anthropomorphic imaginations, easy for divine omnipotence. By an exercise of creative power God caused the physical universe to exist, and in the course of countless ages to bring forth within it organic life, and finally to produce out of organic life personal life . . . But the second stage of the creative process is of a different kind altogether. It cannot be performed by omnipotent power as such. For personal life is essentially free and self-directing. It cannot be perfected by divine fiat, but only through the uncompelled responses and willing co-operation of human individuals in their actions and reactions in the world in which God has placed them. Men may eventually become the perfected persons whom the New Testament calls 'children of God,' but they cannot be created ready-made as this.

The value-judgment that is implicitly being invoked here is that one who has attained to goodness by meeting and eventually mastering temptations, and thus by rightly making responsible choices in concrete situations, is good in a richer and more valuable sense than would be one created *ab initio* in a state of either innocence or of virtue. In the former case, which is that of the actual moral achievements of mankind, the individual's goodness has within it the strength of temptations overcome, a stability based upon an accumulation of right choices, and a positive and responsible character that comes from the investment of costly personal effort. I suggest, then, that it is an ethically reasonable judgment, even though in the nature of the case not one that is capable of demonstrative proof, that human goodness slowly built up through personal histories of moral effort has a value in the eyes of the Creator which justifies even the long travail of the soul-making process.[20]

It follows from Hick's immensely enlightening conclusion that we have profoundly underestimated the problem that God took on for Himself when He decided to create finite replicas of His own Spiritual Nature. To the extent that this is so, it follows that we need to gain a full appreciation of these inherent difficulties *before* we will be capable of understanding the problem of evil in its correct light in relation to God.

Interestingly enough, the maker of the old "Star Trek" series, Gene Roddenberry, seems to have been aware of this important metaphysical relationship between human character development and moral evil, as one of his old episodes, called "Return of the Archons," deals with this very issue. In this marvelous story, a master computer named Landru decides to eliminate evil once and for all on its planet by externally controlling the minds and wills of all the planet's inhabitants. At first this outrageous act of control is amazingly successful in eliminating most of the evils on the planet. But alas, this very act of control turns out to have an extremely destructive effect as well: it inadvertently transforms the "people" who are living there into lifeless sheep. Heroically, though, Captain Kirk convinces the computer—which has been programmed to bring about only good for the population—that it is *not* acting in the best interests of the people by controlling their wills. The computer responds by claiming that its actions are "good," since it has eliminated all moral evil on the planet. Kirk, however, convinces the computer that it has actually committed the greatest evil of them all—the destruction of each individual's freedom and creativity—by relentlessly controlling the people's wills and minds. This realization causes the computer to self-destruct, which in turn allows the people on the planet to instantly return to normal.

The crew on the Enterprise, of course, are delighted to see moral "evils," like marital arguments and bar room brawls, return to the planet, because it is a sign that the people are finally back in control of their own lives.

Spock, however, is intrigued by Landru's initial "success" at getting rid of all moral evil on the planet, so he asks the Captain why the clever people of earth—who have suffered such an overabundance of evil throughout their history—have never tried to implement Landru's ingenious "solution" to the problem of moral wickedness. Kirk replies that they were probably just lucky.

This penetrating statement at once reveals our world to be a far better place than is superficially apparent, precisely because the *only* logically possible alternative to moral evil (besides complete non-existence for humanity) is *far* worse overall: the death of free-willed human character. Hence, as long as we humans wish to remain in control of our lives, this world does indeed seem to be one of the best of all possible worlds, not in terms of the number of evils that occur daily here, but in terms of the underlying metaphysical conditions that allow us to be fully human, and therefore fully in control of our own development. The German philosopher Gottfried Leibniz was apparently aware of this important distinction, as he seems to have based his Principle of Radical Optimism—which states that this is in fact the best of all possible worlds—on the underlying metaphysical conditions that are necessary for human existence, and *not* on the number of evils that occur daily in the world *per se*.

The Image and Likeness of God

Surprisingly enough, the preceding discussion regarding the difficulty of humanity's adoption into the Divine Family is entirely Biblical. The book of Genesis tells us in no uncertain terms that Adam and Eve were created in the direct image and likeness of God (Gen. 1:26–27).

Although modern theologians have experienced considerable difficulty deciphering the true meaning of this cryptic passage, the ancient Church fathers concentrated heavily on it. Indeed, Irenaeus, the Bishop of Lyons and one of the early Church's most important theologians, drew a sharp distinction between the image and likeness of God, at least as far as the creation of human beings is concerned. He believed that humans were initially created in the general image of God, but that this image merely constituted a diffuse spiritual *potentiality* that had to be actualized through a lifelong process of growth and religious devotion in order to be fully realized. The goal of this teleological striving, according to Irenaeus, is to grow into the finite "likeness of God," which in modern terms can be referred to as a state of optimal character assembly.

Thus, the chief difference between the image and likeness of God, according to Irenaeus, is nothing other than the full span of human character development that we all must go through in order to become fully individuated. Accordingly, Irenaeus considered Adam and Eve to be spiritually immature children, and he regarded the Fall as a more or less inevitable consequence of their profound immaturity. This is vitally important, because it casts the entire theology surrounding the Fall in a different light. For instead of making sin the Divine Punishment for Adam and Eve's wrongdoing in the Garden of Eden, as Augustine taught in the fifth century, it makes sin an essential ingredient in the overall process of human development. From this point of view, God intended the Fall all along, since it is only through such an act of disobedience that Adam and Eve could have possibly acquired a state of self-attained maturity and responsible personhood for themselves.

Jung, Evil, and the Trinity

Another area in which Jung's beliefs diverged sharply from that of tradition concerns the alleged triune nature of God. As we have seen, Jung believed that the Trinity was an incomplete image of the Godhead, because he believed that it is in the very nature of ontological wholeness for a complete object to possess four sides, and not just three. Jung was supported in this belief by the fact that the physical symbol of wholeness in the human psyche appears to be a four-sided quaternity. Building on this theoretical backdrop, Jung argued that Satan is the missing element in the Divine quaternity. This in fact explains why he was so opposed to an instrumental view of evil throughout his professional career: because he believed that evil is a permanent feature of the Godhead, and not merely a temporary means to a greater good.

To the extent that Jung is correct in this surmisal, it follows that evil must be an intrinsic, and therefore inevitable, feature of cosmic reality. The direct effect of this theoretical scenario, as we have seen, is that evil necessarily becomes enthroned forever in the all-encompassing nature of the Godhead. For insofar as God is the ultimate creative truth in the universe, and insofar as evil is an intrinsic part of God's underlying makeup, then it would seem to follow that evil will always be a part of creaturely existence as such. And indeed, the only way out of this conclusion, on this "Jungian" view, is if God becomes "conscious" enough to be able to restrict the action of His ominous Left Hand upon the lives of His creatures.

The problem with this Jungian conceptualization of the Godhead is that quaternities only apply to finite objects, but God isn't a finite object at all. He is, rather, an infinite object, so a completely different criterion of wholeness could very well end up applying to Him in the end. Indeed, since God is by definition perfect in all respects, there cannot be any genuine evil in Him at all, as we have seen, because this would mar His perfection and He would no longer be God. In this sense the "incomplete" image of the Trinity is an accurate representation of God's true nature, since it omits any hint of evil in His underlying spiritual makeup.

We can even go so far as to conclude that God is the only Being in existence who can possibly have His wholeness represented by a trinity instead of a quaternity, since He is the only Being in the entire universe who is perfect—and therefore sinless—by His very nature. The Bible concurs on this point as well, as it tells us that God is good, and that there is no evil to be found in Him at all (1 John 3:5).

The Incarnation

Jung's view of the Incarnation is equally bizarre and heretical. For as Stephan A. Hoeller has pointed out, Jung believed that God chose to become human, not to save us, but in order to save Himself from His *own* moral imperfection!

[According to Jung], God is still in the process of growing, of developing consciousness. Jung's God is an undifferentiated being, possessing a double nature. The sufferings of Job, as well as his questionings, have led to a significant achievement. The double nature of God, his light and dark aspect, was now revealed, and with the assistance of the human spirit God would have to renew himself. Jung states bluntly that when God discovered that his creature caught up with him, he then decided that it was time for him to become different. The growth and development of God could occur by God coming to consciousness in humanity—in other words, using Christian terminology, by incarnating. God must become man in order to discover what human consciousness is like and to enlighten his own darkness by the light he might discover in the human spirit. The incarnation of God is a step taken by God because of his recognition that it might benefit him to assimilate the superior qualities present in the human soul and spirit.

Like the ancient Gnostics, so Jung the modern Gnostic turns the traditional reasoning of the Judeo-Christian system of thought upside down. Not only does the almighty but unconscious God desire human consciousness, but also Christ did not become man because humans sinned, but because God needed redemption from sin. Jung states unequivocally that God had to become man because he had done man an injustice.[21]

There is absolutely no concrete evidence, however, to support this grossly unorthodox belief. To the contrary, there is a great deal of logical and historical evidence that legislates decisively *against* it. For one thing, it is very hard to see how the infinite Creator of the universe could possibly be inferior in any conceivable way to His human creatures, and this, in turn, makes it exceedingly unlikely that God could have ever wanted to become human in order to acquire some of our more beneficial qualities for Himself. After all, if God has the power to create the human race, and if He has the power to become incarnated within it, one would think that He would *also* have the power to miraculously acquire any human quality that He desires without having to go to all the trouble of being born to a human mother the way the rest of us are.

Indeed, if God were even the slightest bit evil, unconscious, or whatever, it is hard to see how our exceedingly fine-tuned universe could have ever evolved in the first place to the point that it could support biological life, especially for immense periods of time. Therefore, our very existence in a stable, life-supporting universe provides *ipso facto* evidence that God must be an eminently competent Creator, who is in all likelihood perfect in every conceivable way. The rationale behind this assertion is simply that any force or entity that is powerful enough to be able to contrive our entire life-supporting universe *perfectly* the first time around is almost certainly going to be perfect in every other significant capacity as well. To the extent that this is so, there would clearly be no need at all for God to become human in order to perfect Himself, because He would already be perfect in every relevant way.

The historical teachings of Jesus support us in this conclusion, because Jesus repeatedly taught that God is the most perfect Being in the entire universe, and that it is out of God's infinite love for us that we even have a world at all. He also made it perfectly clear that He came to save *us* from our own sins, and *not* the other way around!

This being the case, it is very difficult to see how Jung's ideas regarding the Incarnation could ever be construed as being coherent, let alone true, even in an infinite number of possible worlds.

Conclusion

As one reads Jung's *Answer to Job*, one quickly gets the impression that Jung brought a preexisting personal bias to his interpretation of the Job story. Evidence for this bias can be found throughout his book, since he chooses to interpret each event in Job's life in the most negative theological manner possible. Indeed, were Jung to have confronted the proverbial half full glass of water while he was in this negative frame of mind, he almost certainly would have found it to be half empty.

However, this sort of self-influenced "eisegesis," or reading into the text, is clearly a travesty against the truth of objective interpretation. For as long as we see only what we want to see in the Scriptures, we will *never* be sure of the true meaning that the Biblical writers meant to convey to us. On the other hand, it is often difficult—some would say even impossible—to bring a totally objective means of interpretation to anything, especially the Bible. The numinous subject matter of this ancient book is simply too symbolic and subjectively-oriented for that. Nevertheless, we must constantly strive to interpret the Bible as fairly as possible, because this is the only way that we can ever hope to be able to come to an awareness of its underlying meaning.

It is ironic that the father of modern symbolic interpretation chose to interpret the book of Job with such uncharacteristic literalness, when it was almost certainly meant to be understood in an allegorical fashion. We can take this to mean that Jung was probably motivated by some sort of deep personal bias against the God of the Old Testament, and indeed, Jung hinted at this possibility in his Introduction, where he admitted to being strongly influenced by his emotions when he actually wrote *Answer to Job*.[22]

At the same time, though, it is the book of Job's timeless capacity to stir our emotions that makes it one of the most important pieces of literature ever written. As such, it will undoubtedly continue to influence readers for many years to come.

Notes

1. Jung, *Answer to Job*, p. 17.
2. John Hick, "Remarks," in *Reason and Religion*, Stuart C. Brown, ed., (Ithaca: Cornell University Press, 1977), pp. 125–126).
3. See my book *God and the New Cosmology* (Lanham, MD: Rowman and Littlefield, 1993) for more on this fascinating subject.
4. Jung, *Answer to Job*, p. 13.
5. C.S. Lewis, *The Problem of Pain* (New York: Macmillan, 1962), pp. 31–34.
6. John Hick, "Remarks," *Reason and Religion*, p. 126.
7. This, however, shouldn't be taken to mean that all character-building natural evils are themselves justified *solely* by their ability to build character. A deeper metaphysical reason—such as that which stems from the necessary nature of the Human Essence—is necessary to justify their initial existence, but this doesn't prevent them from having additional developmental functions in the overall world order.
8. Dietrich Bonhoeffer, *The Cost of Discipleship* (New York: Macmillan Publishing Co., 1949), p. 98.
9. Ibid., p. 99.
10. Ibid., p. 100.
11. Ibid., pp. 47–48.
12. Jung, *Answer to Job*, p. 8.
13. Ibid., pp. 10–11.
14. Ibid., p. 10.
15. John A. Sanford: *Evil: The Shadow Side of Reality*, p. 143.
16. Jung, *Answer to Job*, p. 21n.
17. I am indebted to David Ray Griffin for this particular definition of genuine evil.
18. John Hick, *Evil and the God of Love*, pp. 265–266.
19. See John Hick's *Evil and the God of Love*, pp. 272–282.
20. Ibid., pp. 255–256.
21. Stephan A. Hoeller, *Jung and the Lost Gospels* (Wheaton, IL: Quest Books, 1989), pp. 168–169.
22. Jung, *Answer to Job*, p. xv.

Bibliography

Aquinas, Thomas. "The Summa Theologica," *Great Books of the Western World*, Vol. 19, R. M. Hutchins, ed. (Chicago: Encyclopaedia Britannica, 1952).
Ayer, Alfred Jules. *Language Truth and Logic* (Oxford: Oxford University Press, 1936).
Becker, Ernest. *The Denial of Death* (New York: The Free Press, 1973).
Bonhoeffer, Dietrich. *Creation and Fall* (London: SCM Press, 1959).
———. The *Cost of Discipleship* (New York: Macmillan Publishing Co., 1949).
Clift, Wallace B. *Jung and Christianity* (New York: The Crossroad Publishing Co., 1982).
Corey, M.A. *Back to Darwin* (Lanham: MD: University Press of America, 1994).
———. *God and the New Cosmology* (Lanham, MD: Rowman and Littlefield, 1993).
———. *Male Fraud* (Nashville: Winston-Derek Publishers, 1992).
Davis, Stephen T, ed. *Encountering Evil* (Atlanta: John Knox Press, 1981).
Ferguson, Duncan S. *Biblical Hermeneutics* (Atlanta: John Knox Press, 1986).
Flew, Antony, R.M. Hare, and Basil Mitchell, "Theology and Falsification," *New Essays in Philosophical Theology*, Antony Flew and Alasdair MacIntyre, eds. (London: SCM Press, 1955).
Fromm, Erich. *The Anatomy of Human Destructiveness* (New York: Holt, Rinehart, and Winston, 1973).
———. *You Shall Be As Gods* (New York: Fawcett Premier, 1966).
Goodman, Jeffrey. *The Genesis Mystery* (New York: Times Books, 1983).
Griffin, David Ray. *Evil Revisited* (Albany: SUNY Press, 1991).
———. *God, Power, and Evil* (Philadelphia: The Westminster Press, 1976).
———. *God and Religion in the Postmodern World* (Albany: SUNY Press, 1989).
———ed. *Physics and the Ultimate Significance of Time* (Albany: SUNY Press, 1986).
Griffin, David Ray, and Huston Smith. *Primordial Truth and Postmodern Theology* (Albany: SUNY Press, 1989).
Griffin, David Ray, ed. *The Reenchantment of Science*, (Albany: SUNY Press, 1988).
Hick, John. *Evil and the God of Love* (San Francisco: Harper & Row, 1977).
———. "Remarks," in *Reason and Religion*, Stuart C. Brown, ed., (Ithaca: Cornell University Press, 1977)
———. The Second Christianity (London: SCM Press, 1968).
Hoeller, Stephan A. *Jung and the Lost Gospels* (Wheaton, IL: Quest Books, 1989).
James, William. *The Varieties of Religious Experience* (New York: Longman, Green, & Co., 1902).
Janov, Arthur. *The Primal Scream* (New York: G.P. Putnam's Sons, 1970).
Jantsch, Erich. *The Self-Organizing Universe* (Oxford: Pergamon Press, 1980).

Bibliography 145

Jung, C.G. *Answer to Job* (Princeton: Princeton University Press, 1958).
———. *Man and His Symbols* (New York: Dell Publishing Co., 1964).
———. *Psychology and Western Religion* (Princeton: Princeton University Press, 1984).
Kaufmann, Walter, ed. *Existentialism from Dostoevsky to Sartre* (New York: New American Library, 1975).
Lacey, A.R. *A Dictionary of Philosophy* (London: Routledge & Kegan Paul, 1976).
Lewis, C.S. *Mere Christianity* (New York: Macmillan, 1952).
———. *The Problem of Pain* (New York: Macmillan, 1962).
Long, A.A. *Hellenistic Philosophy* (Berkeley: University of California Press, 1974).
May, Rollo. *Psychology and the Human Dilemma* (New York: W.W. Norton & Co., 1967).
Maimonides, Moses. *The Guide for the Perplexed*, transl. M. Friedlander (London: George Routledge & Sons, 1928).
Meyer, Marvin, transl. *The Gospel of Thomas* (San Francisco: HarperCollins, 1992).
Ortega, Jose. *The Origin of Philosophy* (New York: W.W. Norton and Co., 1967).
Pagels, Elaine. *Adam, Eve, and the Serpent* (New York: Random House, 1988).
Peterson, Michael, William Hasker, Bruce Reichenbach, and David Basinger. *Reason & Religious Belief* (Oxford: Oxford University Press, 1991).
Peterson, Michael L., ed. *The Problem of Evil* (Notre Dame: Notre Dame University Press, 1992).
Pike, Nelson, ed. *God and Evil* (Englewood Cliffs, NJ: Prentice-Hall, 1964).
Plantinga, Alvin. *God, Freedom, and Evil* (Grand Rapids: William B. Eerdmanns Publishing Company, 1974).
———. "Religious Belief Without Evidence," in *Rationality and Religious Belief*, C.F. Delaney, ed., (University of Notre Dame Press, 1979).
———. *The Nature of Necessity* (New York: Oxford University Press, 1974).
Pojman, Louis P. *Philosophy of Religion* (Belmont, CA: Wadsworth Publishing Co., 1987).
Reichenbach, Bruce. *Evil and a Good God* (New York: Fordham University Press, 1982).
Rinpoche, Guru. *The Tibetan Book of the Dead*, transl. by Francesca Fremantle and Chögyam Trungpa (Boston: Shambhala, 1987).
Russell, Jeffrey Burton. *Lucifer* (Ithaca, NY: Cornell University Press, 1984).
———. *Mephistopheles* (Ithaca, NY: Cornell University Press, 1986).
———. *Satan* (Ithaca, NY: Cornell University Press, 1981).
———. *The Devil* (Ithaca, NY: Cornell University Press, 1977).
Sanford, John A. *Evil: The Shadow Side of Reality* (New York: Crossroad Publishing Co., 1981).
———. *The Kingdom Within* (San Francisco: Harper & Row, 1987).
Skinner, B.F. *Beyond Freedom and Dignity* (New York: Knopf, 1971).
Smart, Ninian. "Omnipotence, Evil, and Supermen," *Philosophy*, Vol. XXXVI, No. 137 (1961).
Swinburne, Richard. *The Existence of God* (Oxford: Oxford University Press, 1979).
Tennant, F.R. "Cosmic Teleology," *Philosophical Theology*, Vol. II, chapter IV (New York: Cambridge University Press, 1930).

Von Franz, M.L. *Shadow and Evil in Fairy Tales* (Dallas: Spring Publications, 1974).

Walls, Jerry L. *Hell: The Logic of Damnation* (Notre Dame: University of Notre Dame Press, 1992).

Whitney, Barry L. *What Are They Saying About God and Evil?* (New York: Paulist Press, 1989).

Index

Adam, 52, 99, 108, 139, 140
adoption, 66, 102n
Afterlife, 30, 31, 34, 78–82, 95
Amittai, 6
androgyny, 41
anima, 41
animus, 41
Aquinas, St. Thomas, 62, 113, 132, 134
Augustine, St., 3, 72, 83, 84, 108, 113, 132, 134, 140
Auschwitz, 108

bardo state, 78–82
Barth, Karl, 114
Becker, Ernest, 10–11, 78
Bible, 3, 5
  as allegory, 6–7
Bildad the Shuhite, 76, 94
Bonhoeffer, Dietrich, 127–128
Book of Life, 84, 85

Cause and Effect, Law of, 85
Challenger, 45
cheap grace, 127–128
Christ, Jesus, 8, 9, 10, 15–16, 22, 31, 33, 34, 38–39, 40, 41, 57, 71, 73, 74, 75, 78, 81, 89, 90, 92, 94, 110n, 117–118, 119–120, 127–128
Claremont Graduate School, 45
communion, 73–74
contingency, 99–100
cosmology, 121–122
cross, 66, 71, 73, 89, 92, 94, 102n, 118, 121, 127–128

das Nichtige, 114
demon possession, 15–16, 31, 32–33
  developmental stagnation and, 31–32
  repression and, 15–16
depression, 10
Déscartes, Renée, 130
doubt, power of, 122–123
Dostoevsky, Fyodor, 100
dualism, 50, 105
dysteleological evil, 72–73
  self-transformation and, 73–74

ego, 7, 8, 10, 12, 16, 17–18, 20, 21, 27
Egypt, 55
Elihu the Buzite, 121
Eliphaz, 76, 91–92, 93
essentialism, 62
Eve, 52, 61, 99, 108, 139, 140
evil
  aesthetic view of, 72, 134
  catastrophic, 32, 72, 74, 127–128
  developmental interpretation of, 113–115
  dysteleological, 72–73
  instrumental, 45–47, 50–51, 72, 101n, 132–133
  genuine, 45, 50, 133
  growth facilitation and, 71
  knowledge and, 58–64
  metaphysical necessity of, 70–71
  monotheism and, 104–113
  moral, 3, 7, 8, 13–15, 113–115, 137, 138–139
  Murphy's Law and, 43, 70
  natural, 30–35, 56, 69, 124–127, 143n
  natural causation and, 50–64
  origin of, 3, 137, 138–139
  original sin and, 62
  personification of, 57
  privatio boni interpretation of, 45–46, 113–115, 133
  responsibility for, 61
  socialization and, 55–56
  two possible forms of in God, 44–45

faith
  leap of, 11, 24
  salvation by, 87–88
Fall of Humanity, 139–140
fish
  significance of, 22–23
Flew, Antony, 34
free will, 48, 58, 101n, 102n, 108, 110, 112, 124–125, 128, 136–137, 138–139
Freud, Sigmund, 1–3, 12

Garden of Eden, 52, 61, 99, 140
God
  antinomies and, 131–132
  armor of, 52–53
  contributor to worldly evil, 43–46
  dark side of, 48–49, 50, 51, 64, 132
  grace of, 127–128
  image of, 109–110, 135–138
  image vs. likeness of, 139–140
  incarnation of, 141–142
  kingdom of, 21–22, 41, 67, 73–76
  Left Hand of, 43–44, 50, 52, 140
  Logos, 106–107
  monotheistic nature of, 50–51, 133
  omnibenevolence of, 47–48, 51, 108, 109
  omnipotence of, 50, 51, 108, 109, 110–111, 128, 130, 133–134, 136
  omniscience of, 123–124, 130–131
  nature of, 38–39
  response to Job, 96–98
  Satan as missing part of, 44
  triune nature of, 44, 140–141
Griffin, David Ray, 45, 108, 143n

heaven
  behavior and, 64–65, 85–90
  entrance into, 21, 39–40, 42, 75
  kingdom of, 89
  state of mind and, 86–87
hell, 17
  repression and, 78–84
  Tibetan Book of the Dead and, 78–82, 102–103n,
  universalism and, 82–84
Hick, John, 6, 79–80, 82–83, 85, 99, 110–111, 112, 115n, 118–119, 126, 132, 134, 136, 137–138
Hiroshima, 108
Hitler, Adolph, 53
Hoeller, Stephan A., 141–142
homeopathy, 47
Human Essence, 46, 47, 49, 50, 51, 63, 103n, 105, 107, 109, 113, 143n
humility, 25

individuation, 7, 17, 70, 72, 74, 89–90, 119, 120, 121, 127, 128, 139–140
  evil and, 71–72
  value of, 14

Irenaeus, 139–140
Islam, 50, 104, 119, 133

James, St., 88–89
Janov, Arthur, 10, 21, 26, 74
Job,
  blamelessness of, 37–40
  calamities of, 42
  developmental status of, 38–40
  identity of, 37
John, St., 84
Jonah,
  author of, 5
  historicity of, 5–6
Judaism, 50, 104, 119, 133
judgment, 64–65, 84–90
Jung, C.G., 1, 2, 7, 26, 31, 37, 41, 43, 44, 45, 116–117, 121–123, 128–134, 140–143

Kant, Immanual, 103n
karma, 69, 79–82, 85, 95–96, 124
Kierkegaard, Søren, 10–11, 24
Kirk, Captain, 13–14, 138–139
knowledge, 58–64
Kunkel, Fritz, 1

Lake of Fire, 84
Landru, 138–139
Lazarus, Parable of, 86–87
laziness, 62–63
Left Hand of God, 43–44, 50, 52, 140
Leibniz, G.W., 114, 132, 139
Lewis, C.S., 105, 124–125
Lisbon, 30
Lost Coin, Parable of, 9
Lost Sheep, Parable of, 84
luck, 19

Mackie, J.L., 34, 101n
Maslow, Abraham, 7
metaphysical necessity, 108–110, 113, 114
  definition of, 103n
Murphy's Law, 43, 52, 70
morality, 62
Mussolini, Benito, 53

Natural Causation, Law of, 42–43, 52, 58, 66, 67, 68, 126
Nazi Germany, 56, 65, 127

necessity, 99–100, 108–110, 113, 114
necrophilia, 53
neurosis, 9
Nineveh, 6, 7, 11, 16, 25–26, 27, 28, 29, 30, 36n
non-being, 114–115
　absolute, 114
　meontic, 114

Occam's Principle of Theoretical Economy, 54
O Felix Culpa, 99
omnipotence, 50, 51, 83, 105, 108, 109
　second-order, 101n
omniscience, 123–124, 130–131
order, 14
original sin, 62

pain
　negative reinforcement and, 63
　purgative force, 71
　self-punishment and, 71
　self-purification and, 71
　trial by fire and, 64
Pascal, Blaise, 59
past lives, 69
Paul, St., 41, 53, 66, 102n
Peck, M. Scott, 62
perfection, 40–41
Peter, St., 73
Pharisees, 39–40, 117, 119
Plantinga, Alvin, 62, 101n
Plato, 62
pleasure principle, 12
pluralism, 119–120
Popper, Karl, 136
pride, 25, 95–98, 129
Primal Therapy, 26, 74
Principle of Radical Optimism, 139
process theism, 103n, 108–109, 115n
Purgatory, 82

quantum field, 106
quantum mechanics, 106
quaternities, 44, 140–141

redemption, 2, 120
Reichenbach, Bruce, 36n, 72, 101n, 115n
repentance, 33–34

Return of the Archons, 138–139
Roddenberry, Gene, 138

salvation, 2, 82–84, 85–90
　by faith, 88–89
　pluralistic view of, 119–120
　sanctification, 87–88
Sanford, John A., 1, 2, 9, 20, 38, 39, 74–75, 81, 85, 90, 104, 107, 132
Santorini, 55
Satan, 32, 42–44, 49–50, 51–59, 64–69, 116–117, 122–127, 133, 140
　archetype of real-world causality
　archetype of self-purification, 65
　external being, 104
　missing element of Divine quaternity, 44–45
scribes, 40
Second Law of Thermodynamics, 14–15
Self, 7, 9, 12, 16–17, 18, 19, 20–21, 26–27, 82
self-actualization, 7, 118
self-punishment, 17, 28, 68
self-purification, 15
serpent, 61, 108
Shadow, 7–11, 16, 20–21, 26, 27, 44
　contribution to personality, 12–15
　evil aspects of, 13–14
　fear and, 77
　goodness of, 14
　identity of, 12–15
　Star Trek and, 13–14
　wholeness and, 41
Socrates, 137
Spain, 11
Spock, 139
Star Trek, 13–14, 138–139
Stoics, 43, 106
suffering, 33
　arranged by God, 69–70
superego, 19
Swinburne, Richard, 72, 115n, 132

Tarshish, 11, 27
theism,
　Freudian view of, 1–3
Thomas, Gospel of, 8–9, 41, 49
Tibetan Book of the Dead, 78–82, 102–103n
Trinity, 140–141

universalism, 82–84

Way of Truthful Life, 120
Wedding Feast, Parable of, 75–76
whales, 5–6

wisdom, 59–64, 101–102n
World War II, 15, 127

Yahweh, 123, 130

Zophar, 76

About the Author

M.A. Corey is the author of six other books, including *God and the New Cosmology, Back to Darwin,* and *Evolution and the Dawn of Creation.* He is a Summa Cum Laude graduate of West Virginia State College and an alumnus of the Claremont Graduate School, where he studied the philosophy of science and religion. He also studied human biological science at the West Virginia University School of Medicine. An avid proponent of old-style natural theology, his goal is to help stimulate a much-needed reconciliation between the scientific and religious communities.